# THE
# LITTLE
# BOOK
## OF
# MURDER

NEIL R. STOREY

*For Anne*

First published 2013

The History Press
The Mill, Brimscombe Port
Stroud, Gloucestershire, GL5 2QG
www.thehistorypress.co.uk

© Neil R. Storey, 2013

The right of Neil R. Storey to be identified as the Author
of this work has been asserted in accordance with the
Copyright, Designs and Patents Act 1988.

British Library Cataloguing in Publication Data.
A catalogue record for this book is available from the British Library.

ISBN 978 0 7524 6994 2

Typesetting and origination by The History Press
Printed in Great Britain

# CONTENTS

# INTRODUCTION

The cases of murder spattered across the pages of history provide a dark mirror for so many aspects of the less seemly world of the past. Tales of the ultimate crime often live on in the stories told about a locality or even murders that became notorious to the whole nation, even infamous across the world; they can even be popular in the memory of generations to come after the event. Unfortunately, the re-telling and the frailties of the human memory have often meant the facts of cases – the names of those involved, number of victims, or events surrounding the crime – have been distorted, confused or simply forgotten.

This book does not attempt to list every infamous murder, nor does it pretend to be a concise almanac of such crimes; instead, it is aimed at all those armchair crime buffs who, like me, occasionally scratch their heads and try to recall the basic facts of some notorious or curious case of murder from the past. It is also based on the many questions and enquiries I have received after lectures and in letters I have received from the readers of my books over my twenty years as a crime historian and includes many of the cases that have intrigued me over those years, particularly those that contain some curious twist, a significant point of law or milestone of detection or forensics within it, or remain an unsolved mystery.

In this volume you will discover such gobbets of murderous information as: there was a murder between rival elephant keepers at London Zoo in 1928; not just one but two murders have been committed on Potters Bar Golf Course in Hertfordshire; what was 'The Otterburn Mystery' and how

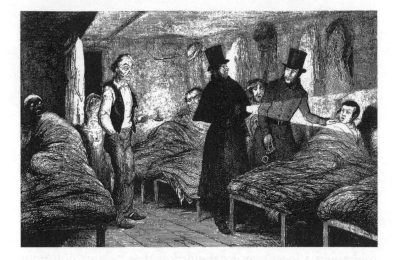

many 'Brides' did George Joseph Smith drown in the bath? Learn what was found down the drains of a house in the leafy suburb of Cranley Gardens in Muswell Hill in 1983, discover who was the first internet serial killer, find out where there is a book charting an account of an infamous murder – bound in the murderer's own skin, and learn of some of the strangest weapons that have been used by murderers, items as diverse as a tubular chair, a gas ring dismantled from a cooker and even a 10lb jar of pickles.

You can use this book to create a crime quiz, you can read it from cover to cover or dip into it as you please, there are no rules and you will soon see the ease with which one can enliven conversation, intrigue friends and even impress a few ardent crime fans with the knowledge you have obtained from this book.

*Neil R. Storey, 2013*

# 1

# MURDEROUS BRITAIN

## NORTH & MIDLANDS

*Mrs Maybrick*
One of the most sensational trials of a woman in the late nineteenth century was that of Florence 'Florie' Maybrick, a pretty American girl from a good family. She married James Maybrick, an English cotton broker, some twenty-three years her senior, in 1881. They made their home at Battlecrease House in the Liverpool suburb of Aigburth. Maybrick was not easy to live with; he was known to take concoctions of drugs and maintained a number of mistresses, one of whom bore him five children. The disenchanted Florie had a few clandestine liaisons of her own, including a dalliance with her husband's brother, Edwin. James heard of her affair with local businessman Alfred Brierley and after a violent row, during which he assaulted Florie, Maybrick demanded a divorce.

In April 1889, Florie bought flypapers that she knew contained arsenic and soaked them in a bowl of water to extract the poison for cosmetic use. On 27 April 1889 James was taken ill, the doctor was called for and he was treated for acute dyspepsia, but his condition declined and he died on 11 May 1889. Suspicious of the cause of death, Maybrick's brothers requested that James' body be examined. Traces of arsenic were detected, not enough to prove fatal, but they were present and Florie was arrested and tried for murder at the Liverpool Assizes in

THE MAYBRICK POISONING MYSTERY: GUILTY OR NOT GUILTY?

MRS FLORENCE MAYBRICK IN HER CELL.

July 1889. The evidence against her was flimsy – there was no way of proving Florie had administered the arsenic to James but it seems her private affairs drew enough condemnation and she was found guilty, more for lack of morals than for direct evidence of murder. Florie was sentenced to death, which was eventually respited in favour of penal servitude. Her case became a *cause célèbre*, but she was only released – after serving fourteen years – in January 1904. Florie returned to the United States and died in poverty in 1941. Among her few remaining possessions was discovered a tatty family bible, and pressed between its yellowed pages was a scrap of paper which had written upon it, in faded ink, the directions for soaking flypapers for use as a beauty treatment.

### The Strange Death of Sidney Marston

Marjorie Yellow and Emily Thay were sisters, one in her late teens the other in her early twenties. Both had already been married and, scandalously for the time, both had separated from their husbands. Emily was spending the weekend with her sister, who was now living with another man named Herbert Gwinnell at Willow Crescent on Cannon Hill in Birmingham. Shortly after 7.30 p.m. on 24 October 1932, Emily rushed out onto the street screaming 'Murder!' Marjorie followed, asking for help to put a man out of their house. As a passer-by ran up, a man stumbled out of the house; he had been stabbed in the chest and with his dying breath gasped, 'I have done nothing,' before he collapsed onto the porch and died.

The sisters were charged with murder but the evidence produced against them was both confusing and conflicting. The dead man was identified as Sidney Marston, who was described as a thickset young man who could look after himself. There was not a trace of a defensive wound on his person or sign of a struggle and in his pocket was the blade of a knife; the handle lay nearby. Yellow said Marston had stabbed himself; there was talk of a missing 10s note, which was found in Marston's pocket. Yellow denied knowing Marston, but later said she had met him at a dance; other casual remarks she was recorded as making were, 'He's only shamming. He's done that before,' and, most curiously, 'They don't hang women do they?' Even the great Sir Bernard Spilsbury, Home Office pathologist, could not attribute an opinion of blame or guilt to any of the parties, and a verdict of not guilty was passed on the sisters.

## Nurse Waddingham

Known in the annals of crime as 'Nurse' Waddingham, Dorothea Waddingham had no formal training as a nurse, and what medical knowledge she did have was probably obtained when she worked as a ward maid at an infirmary in Burton-on-Trent. Waddingham had a murky past and had served prison terms for fraud and theft. She gained her appointment as matron only because she and her husband turned their home on Devon Drive, Nottingham, into a private nursing home for elderly and infirm patients. Two patients, a Mrs Baguley and her daughter, both of who had named Waddingham as a beneficiary in their wills, died a short time apart. Suspicions arose and a post-mortem examination was ordered on the body of the daughter – over three grains of morphine were found in her internal organs. Mrs Baguley's body was then exhumed and it was found that she too had died from morphine poisoning. Tried and found guilty, Waddingham was executed on 16 April 1936 by Thomas Pierrepoint at Winson Green Prison, Birmingham.

## The Green Bicycle Case

On the evening of 5 July 1919 Joseph Cowell was driving his cattle along Gartree Road in the Leicestershire village of Little Stretton. He came to a small dip in the road and saw a young woman on the ground, with a bicycle beside her. Concerned she had come off her bike and been hurt, Cowell went to inspect more closely and found to his horror that she had been shot just below the left eye. Matters were reported to the police and she was soon identified as Bella Wright, aged twenty-one, a nightshift worker in a Leicester factory. Investigations revealed that earlier in the evening she had biked over to see her uncle in a nearby village and with her was a man she had described as a stranger, but when she left, her uncle noticed that they rode off together. Despite a high-profile police investigation, the only clue was that the man had ridden a green bicycle.

No further clues emerged until 23 February 1920, when a canal boatman, taking a load to the factory where Bella had worked, dredged up a green bicycle. A subsequent search of the canal found a revolver holster and bullets.

Green bicycles were rare in those days and this one had certain features which led police to identify the owner as Ronald Light. Light was brought to trial in a classic case where legendary counsels Marshall Hall (for the defence) and Norman Birkett (for the prosecution) were to meet for the first time. Light made a good impression in the witness box, and much was made of the shell shock he suffered during the First World War. He admitted he should have come forward earlier – he convincingly argued that anyone in his position may have reacted similarly in the same situation, but swore that he had turned off the road at the junction before the murder site. He was acquitted, to popular acclaim, and the

*Telephone 357 and 862.*

# LEICESTERSHIRE CONSTABULARY.

# £5 REWARD.

At 9-20 p.m., 5th instant, the body of a woman, since identified as that of ANNIE BELLA WRIGHT, was found lying on the Burton Overy Road, Stretton Parva, with a bullet wound through the head, and her bicycle lying close by.

Shortly before the finding of the body the deceased left an adjacent village in company of a man of the following description :—

Age 35 to 40 years, height 5 ft. 7 in. to 5 ft. 9 in.; apparently usually clean shaven, but had not shaved for a few days, hair turning grey, broad full face, broad build, said to have squeaking voice and to speak in a low tone.

Dressed in light Rainproof Coat with green plaid lining, grey mixture jacket suit, grey cap, collar and tie, black boots, and wearing cycle clips.

Had bicycle of following description, *viz.*:—Gent's B.S.A., green enamelled frame, black mudguards, usual plated parts, up-turned handle bar, 3-speed gear, control lever on right of handle bar, lever front brake, back-pedalling brake worked from crank and of unusual pattern, open centre gear case, *Brooke's* saddle with spiral springs of wire cable. The 3-speed control had recently been repaired with length of new cable.

**Thorough enquiries are earnestly requested at all places where bicycles are repaired.**

If met with the man should be detained, and any information either of the man or the bicycle wired or telephoned to E. HOLMES, ESQ., CHIEF CONSTABLE OF COUNTY, LEICESTER, or to SUPT L BOWLEY, COUNTY POLICE STATION, LEICESTER.

*County Constabulary Office,*
*Leicester, 7th July, 1919.*

question of whether Light committed the murder remains one that is still hotly debated among criminologists and crime historians today.

# SOUTH

### The Richmond Poisoning

In 1858, Dr Thomas Smethurst of Richmond, Surrey, and his wife took in a lodger, a spinster named Isabella Bankes. When he discovered her wealth, Smethurst declared his love for Bankes. They soon moved out together and bigamously married. In March 1859 Isabella was taken ill and Smethurst called in medical help. Samples from one of her evacuations were sent for tests and arsenic was detected. Meanwhile, Miss Bankes drew up a will leaving everything to Smethurst; however, when she died, Smethurst was arrested for her murder.

Small quantities of antimony were found in her body during the post-mortem, but she had recently been administered a variety of medicines which could have contained that particular element. Smethurst was found guilty but was not given the death sentence; the medical evidence conflicted, the evacuation contained the arsenic but none was actually found in her body, and medical experts argued that Miss Bankes had been ill for quite some time before her fatal illness. Smethurst was granted a pardon, only to be jailed for bigamy. He was, however, successful in proving Isabella's will in his favour!

### Murder at the Metropole

Sidney Harry Fox had been a petty swindler since boyhood and by the 1920s had already served a prison sentence for theft. Fox and his mother appeared affluent and lived well, travelling around Britain and staying in high-class hotels before flitting without paying their bills. In April 1929 Fox persuaded his mother to make her will, of which he would be the main beneficiary, and the following month he increased the accident insurance policy on her life. The pair checked into the Metropole

Hotel in Margate, Kent, in October 1929. On the night of 23 October Sidney Fox raised the alarm after discovering his mother's room on fire. Mrs Fox was removed from the room, but had died in the fire. The doctor initially certified her death as one of suffocation and shock and her funeral went ahead, but insurance assessors were suspicious and had her body exhumed. The post-mortem was conducted by Home Office pathologist Sir Bernard Spilsbury, who discovered a bruise on her larynx and no soot in her lungs, therefore concluding that she had been strangled before the fire had started. Thirty-one-year-old Sidney Fox was arrested and charged with the murder of his mother. He was found guilty and hanged at Maidstone Prison by executioner Robert Baxter on 8 April 1930.

*Sweet Fanny Adams*
On 24 August 1867 the sun was shining down and it was a beautiful day for children to play outside. In the early afternoon three young girls, Minnie Warner, aged eight and sisters Lizzie, aged seven, and Fanny Adams, also aged eight, were walking up Tanhouse Lane towards Flood Meadow in Alton, Hampshire, when they encountered solicitors' clerk twenty-nine-year-old Frederick Baker. He was friendly to the girls and gave Minnie and Lizzie three halfpence and sent them away for sweets. He then offered Fanny a ha'penny to go with him. When she refused he picked her up and carried her away towards Shalden, out of sight into a hop field. He then butchered the poor girl; he cut off her legs and cut open her torso, before ripping out most of her internal organs and scattering them about. Next, he cut off her head and gouged out her eyes, which he threw into a nearby river. He then cleaned himself up and walked off as if nothing had happened.

By 4 p.m. the other girls had returned home but there was still no sign of Fanny, so her mother and neighbours went to look for her. At 5.30 p.m. a neighbour, Mrs Gardiner, saw Baker and asked him what he had been up to. He admitted giving the girls money but claimed that Fanny had left him to join the others. Gardiner was not entirely happy with his answers but she respected him as a clerk and thought him to be honest.

Baker then went for a drink at the Swan Inn. A short while later Fanny's remains were discovered and the town went into uproar. The police traced Baker to the solicitor's office where he worked, and when he was removed from the building he had to be protected from the mob which had gathered outside.

When the police searched Baker's office a couple of days later they uncovered his diary, which contained the chilling entry for Saturday 24 August – '... killed a young girl. It was fine and hot.' On examination of his clothes, traces of blood were found, along with two small knives, one of which showed traces of bloodstains. At his trial, attempts to mitigate Baker's actions were made by arguing for insanity, but the jury were unconvinced and after deliberating for just fifteen minutes returned a verdict of 'guilty'. The case had drawn massive public interest and Baker was hanged in front of a crowd of 5,000 outside Winchester Prison on 24 December 1867, the prison's last public execution. A short while after these horrific events, rations were changed to include tinned mutton for British sailors; they were unimpressed, and the derisory joke arose that the meat must be the chunks of 'Sweet Fanny Adams'. The term, meaning as good as useless or nothing at all, has been in parlance ever since.

# EAST

## The Burnham Poisoners
Two sudden deaths, initially blamed on a mystery 'sickness', occurred in quick succession within the Frary household in early March 1835, leaving poor Catherine Frary, aged forty, a widow and mourning the loss of a child. Two weeks later neighbour Mary Taylor, wife of forty-five-year-old Peter Taylor, a journeyman cobbler, was taken violently ill and died in the course of the afternoon and evening of 12 March. Mr Cremer, the local surgeon, had attended Mary in her dying hours and his suspicions were aroused. The contents of Mary's stomach were analysed and found to contain arsenic. At the inquest it was suggested that Peter Taylor had been 'associated' with Frances 'Fanny' Billing, aged forty-six, who was described as 'a woman of loose character'. Investigations revealed that Frary and Billing had entered into a pact whereby each would murder the obstacle to their happiness and love.

Brought before the county assizes, Frary was charged with administering poison to Mary Taylor with Billing as an accessory before the fact. The second indictment charged them both with murdering Robert Frary. The death of the child was not mentioned in the charges. It was proved both women had purchased poison and their motives were suggested. Neither prisoner said a word in their defence nor called any witnesses. After a short deliberation the jury found both women guilty. Frances Billing and Catherine Frary dictated their confessions in their condemned cells, adding that they had not only mixed arsenic with Mr Frary's porter and gruel but with his pills, and that it took four doses of the poison to kill him. Their execution, conducted in public in front of Norwich Castle on 10 August 1835, proved to be the last public double execution conducted in the county and they remain the last women to be hanged in Norfolk.

### The Suffolk Tragedy

When thirty-nine-year-old John Smith married his second wife Elizabeth, aged twenty-seven, she became stepmother to John's three children – a role which she did not much care for. In mitigation, John worked hard and probably had little time or patience for his children; even so, no caring parent would have stood by as his children starved and bruises and wheals appeared on their bodies. It emerged from the witness statements of family members and neighbours that the children were locked in sheds, hung up by their feet or hoisted by a rope around their middles – it was by this treatment

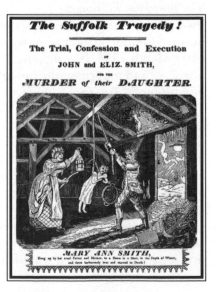

**The Suffolk Tragedy!**

The Trial, Confession and Execution
OF
JOHN and ELIZ. SMITH,
FOR THE
**MURDER** *of their* **DAUGHTER.**

*MARY ANN SMITH,*

Hung up by her cruel Father and Mother, to a Beam in a Shed, in the Depth of Winter, and there barbarously beat and starved to Death!

that the eldest child, eight-year-old Mary Ann died. Her tiny, starved body could take no more hoistings and she died through lack of food and mortification at the hands of John and Elizabeth. John Wright, the Constable of Halesworth, was summoned; the evidence was all too clear and the couple were taken into custody. At the assizes the jury was out for barely five minutes before finding John and Elizabeth guilty. The Smiths were hanged together at Ipswich Gaol on 23 March 1812.

## The Blazing Car Murder

Alfred Arthur Rouse was a commercial traveller, with what he liked to refer to as a 'harem' of women dotted across the country, one of whom he had bigamously married. This situation was not cheap, especially when one of his 'harem' presented him with a child – a result of their relationship – and a child support order was granted, with another case pending, and another woman expecting him to make good on his promise to marry her. Rouse wanted to disappear and struck upon the idea of faking his death by torching his car and putting the body of a transient, who would not be missed, inside it to take his place. He committed this act in the small hours of 6 November 1930 on Hardingstone Lane, about three miles from Northampton. Despite fleeing from the scene, Rouse was soon traced and arrested.

In his statement, Rouse claimed that he had picked the stranger up during a drive to Leicester. He had stopped the car to relieve himself and while doing so, the stranger lit a cigarette and the car burst in flames. His story was not believed and his antics with his 'harem' did not endear him to anyone. The forensic evidence was against him as well; the nut that controlled the flow of petrol in the car had clearly been forced to allow petrol to flow dangerously into the motor. With prosecution for the Crown led by Norman Birkett, the evidence was eloquently presented against him and it came as no surprise when Rouse was found guilty. He was executed at HMP Bedford on 31 March 1931. Rouse confessed to his crime shortly before his execution, stating that he had got the stranger drunk on whiskey, strangled him, doused him in petrol and then set the car on fire by a petrol trail from ten yards away. The unfortunate man who was so horrifically burned in the car remains unidentified.

### Priscilla Biggadyke

The case of Priscilla Biggadyke remains one of the most notorious in the annals of Lincolnshire criminal history. Richard Biggadyke, aged thirty, was a well sinker living in Mareham-le-Fen with his wife Priscilla. Although low in station they had a tolerable standard of living and shared their house, although there was just one room for sleeping, with three children and two male lodgers, one of which was Thomas Proctor, a rat catcher.

Richard was in the habit of leaving his wife in bed when he went to work and was suspicious that she had been unfaithful with Proctor; he had even begun to think that their youngest child was, in fact, the result of a liaison between Proctor and his wife.

On 30 September 1868 Richard sat down to a meal of mutton followed by shortcake, which had been made by Priscilla. Within ten minutes he was stricken by retching and excruciating pain in his stomach; he died in agony the following morning. Analysis of his stomach by Professor Taylor revealed a large quantity of arsenic. When suspicion fell upon Priscilla, who had made comments to the effect that she wished her husband dead, she immediately tried to deflect them onto Proctor. She said that she had seen him put a white powder into a teacup and the medicine ordered for her husband and he was taken into custody. Confusing statements given by Priscilla did not help her case and she was placed in the House of Correction, and it was not long before both Proctor and Priscilla were brought before the assizes. The case against Proctor did not hold up and he was acquitted – the main thrust of the prosecution was now turned upon Priscilla. She was found guilty of the murder and was sentenced to death, all on quite circumstantial evidence.

Despite her family and the prison chaplain imploring her to confess, Priscilla protested her innocence all the way to the gallows at Lincoln Castle on 28 December 1868. Her last words to the executioner, Thomas Askern, were, 'Oh! You won't hang me!' just before the traps opened.

In 1882, Thomas Proctor, laying on his deathbed, confessed that he did indeed commit the murder.

### The Southend Murder

James Canham Read was a middle-aged cashier at the Royal Albert Docks in London. He had a wife and eight children; he also had a string of mistresses, one of which was a pretty young woman named Florence Dennis, aged eighteen. Their romantic liaisons resulted in her becoming pregnant and she had no hesitation in naming Read as the father. She wrote to him asking what he proposed to do about it and he arranged to meet her in secret in Prittlewell, Southend, on 24 June 1894. When she did not return, her concerned sister, who, incidentally, had also been one of Read's mistresses, wrote to him to enquire if he could shed some light on Florence's whereabouts. Read panicked, stole money from his office and fled with another mistress to Mitcham in Surrey.

Meanwhile, Florence's body was recovered from a field at Prittlewell. She had been shot. Read was traced and arrested, before being tried and found guilty of her murder at the Chelmsford Assizes – he duly paid the ultimate price at Springfield Gaol in Chelmsford on 4 December 1894.

Later, J. Holt Schooling, a member of Lord Egerton's Committee on the Mental and Physical Condition of Children, was to comment that Read had the face of a murderer; 'Not even the most casual observer can fail to see it ... (his face causes) a feeling of aversion and distrust'.

## The Murder of PC Gutteridge

During the early hours of 27 September 1927, PC George Gutteridge stopped a motor car (which was later discovered to be stolen) to enquire the business of the occupants at such an early hour. He was met with two shots from a revolver. Mortally wounded he fell to the ground, only for the gunman to get out of the car and shoot him twice more, once through each eye. As the news of Gutteridge's murder broke in the national press a country was left horrified.

Police enquiries soon led them to the garage of forty-nine-year-old Frederick Guy Browne, and when the premises were searched two Webley revolvers were discovered. Until recently, William Henry Kennedy, aged thirty-six, had been living in the back room of the garage; he was traced and arrested in Liverpool. He gave a statement in which he admitted helping to steal the car, as well as being in it with Browne when he had shot PC Gutteridge. Browne swore it was Kennedy who had stolen the car and shot the policeman; he claimed to have been at home with his wife.

This was one of the first cases in which the science of ballistics played a key role. The pistols found in the garage were proven to have fired the fatal shots, and Browne and Kennedy were both found guilty of murder and sentenced to death. They were hanged by Robert Baxter and Thomas Pierrepoint at Pentonville and Wandsworth respectively on 31 May 1928.

## The Raleigh Bath Chair Murder

Archibald Brown, of Rayleigh, Essex, suffered from paralysis of the spine following a motorbike accident. His mobility had gradually decreased over the years until he lost all movement in his legs in 1942. This, however, did not stop him from being a tyrannical husband and father who bullied and verbally abused his wife and two sons, making their lives a misery.

On the afternoon of 23 July 1943, the resident nurse, Nurse Mitchell, and Mr Brown set out on one of their regular constitutionals. About a mile from the house Mr Brown stopped to have a smoke. Nurse Mitchell lit the cigarette and, after straightening the blankets, moved to the back of the wheelchair when she was suddenly thrown to the ground by an explosion. Dazed but miraculously unharmed, she looked up and saw that Mr Brown had been blasted in half by the force of the blast. The police examination of the crime scene revealed that the explosion had been caused by a Hawkins No.75 Grenade Mine – an anti-tank device used by infantrymen – secreted underneath the wheelchair. Eric Brown, Archibald's eldest son, had been trained in the use of the Hawkins when he had volunteered for the army, and such mines were kept at his company HQ. When interviewed at the Essex Assizes, he appeared unrepentant and unable to comprehend that he had committed murder. A testimony was given by nerve specialist Dr Rowland Hill, who diagnosed Eric as having schizophrenia. Accordingly, a judgement of 'guilty but insane' was passed and Eric Brown was committed to a mental institution.

### Murder on the Golf Course – twice over!
The Potters Bar Golf Course in Hertfordshire has been the scene of not just one but two murders. The first occurred on 19 November 1947, when forty-five-year-old railway worker Albert Welch went out for a walk from his house in Cranbourne Crescent. His battered and dismembered body was discovered months later – in May 1948 – by boys searching for lost golf balls in foliage surrounding a pond adjacent to the 7th green. His killer remains unknown.

Only a few years later, forty-six-year-old Elizabeth Currell was walking her dog on the golf course on the evening of

29 April 1955. When the dog returned home alone, her husband went looking for her. He traced Elizabeth's usual route but did not find her and so reported her missing. A police officer discovered her body the next morning in the rough by the 17th tee. She had been felled from a blow from a heavy iron tee marker and strangled with a stocking. The tee marker lay discarded nearby and a portion of a bloody palm print was found upon its handle. The police then undertook the massive task of taking 9,000 palm prints from local residents. After wading through about 4,000 prints a match was found with Michael Queripel, a local council clerk. He pleaded guilty to the murder and was ordered to be detained at Her Majesty's pleasure.

# WEST COUNTRY

### The Road Hill House Murder

In the sleepy village of Road in Wiltshire, the finely built Road Hill House, home of wealthy factory inspector Samuel Saville Kent, was thrown into turmoil at about 7.15 a.m. on 30 June 1860. The family nursemaid, Elizabeth Gough, discovered that three-year-old Francis Saville Kent was missing from his cot. The alarm was raised and a search of the house and gardens ensued. Francis's body was discovered, forced deep into the vault of a disused privy in the grounds of the house. He had a stab wound to the chest and his throat had been cut with such force that his head was almost severed from his body. Initial suspicion fell upon his nursemaid; she was arrested but released after questioning. Local authorities needed to be seen to be doing all they could to resolve the case and asked Scotland Yard for an officer to head the investigation; on their second request, Detective Inspector Jonathan Whicher was dispatched. His investigations saw suspicion fall upon sixteen-year-old Constance Kent, Francis's half-sister, but the evidence against her was circumstantial. After a hearing before the local magistrates she was released on bail and the case was dropped.

The case attracted considerable public sympathy for Constance, and Whicher was heavily criticised in the press – his reputation never recovered. Five years later, Constance Kent confessed to the murder. She was subsequently sentenced to death but this was commuted to twenty years' penal servitude. She was released from prison in 1881 and spent the rest of her life in obscurity.

## The Tregonissey Poisoning

Thirty-six-year-old Ernest Edward Black earned a precarious living as an insurance salesman in Tregonissey, near St Austell in Cornwall. By 1921 he was in debt and no longer in love with his wife, Annie – he wanted out. Black purchased 2oz of poison 'for killing rats' and signed the poisons register at a chemist in St Austell.

On 30 October 1921 he added this deadly powder to his wife's breakfast; Annie was struck ill soon after. The doctor was summoned and attended her over the next few days. As her condition appeared to improve, Ernest Black went off on his bicycle, saying he was going for cigarettes, and did not return. Annie died a few days later.

Initially it was thought she had died from gastro-enteritis but the doctor had his suspicions and a post-mortem was ordered, which revealed traces of arsenic in her body. A manhunt was launched and Black was traced to Liverpool, after the proprietor of the hotel where he was staying recognised him from the photo published in the press. When the police arrived at Black's door he would not admit them into his room, so they had to force the door. He was found with a self-inflicted gash to his throat from his penknife. Brought back to Cornwall, he was tried and found guilty of murder. Black was executed at Exeter Prison on 24 March 1922.

## Inspiration for Tess

Elizabeth Martha Brown became the last woman to be executed in public in Dorset, when she was hanged outside Dorchester Prison on 9 August 1856. Under sentence of death, she wrote her confession in the condemned cell:

My husband John Anthony Brown, deceased, came home on Sunday morning, the 6th July at 2 o'clock in liquor and was sick. He had no hat on. I asked him what he had done with his hat. He abused me and said 'What is it to you, d___n you? He then asked for some cold tea. I said that I had none, but would make him some warm. He replied 'Drink that yourself, and be d___d'. I then said 'What makes you so cross? Have you been at Mary Davis's?' He then kicked out the bottom of the chair upon which I had been sitting. We continued quarrelling until 3 o'clock, when he struck me a severe blow on the side of my head, which confused me so much that I was obliged to sit down. Supper was on the table and he said 'Eat it yourself, and be d___d'. At the same time he reached down for the mantelpiece a heavy horse whip with a plain end and struck me across the shoulders with it three times. Each time I screamed out. I said 'If you strike me again, I will cry Murder'. He retorted 'If you do, I will knock your brains out through the window'. He also added 'I hope I shall find you dead in the morning'. He then kicked me on the left side which caused me much pain, and he immediately stooped down to untie his boots. I was such enraged and in an ungovernable passion, on being so abused and struck, I directly seized an hatchet which was lying close to where I sat and which I had been using to break coal with to keep up the fire and keep his supper warm, and with it [the hatchet] I struck him several violent blows on the head, I could not say how many. He fell at the first blow on his head, with his face towards the fireplace. He never spoke or moved afterwards. As soon as I had done it I wished I had not, and would have given the world not to have done it. I had never struck him before after all his ill treatment but when he hit me so hard at this time, I was almost out of my senses and hardly knew what I was doing.

The execution was watched by a crowd of between 3,000 and 4,000 spectators, including a sixteen-year-old Thomas Hardy, who, in a letter written seventy years later, recalled the execution vividly, but commented that he was, in retrospect, 'ashamed' to have been present; 'My only excuse being that I was but a youth, and had to be in town at that time for other reasons ... I remember what a fine figure she showed against the sky as she hung in the misty rain, and how the tight black silk gown set off her shape as she wheeled half-round and back.' The vision stayed with him and provided part of the inspiration for *Tess of the D'Urbervilles*, which ends with Tess being hanged for stabbing to death the man who ruined her.

## The Man They Could Not Hang

On 23 February 1885, public executioner James Berry was employed at Exeter Prison to carry out the execution of nineteen-year-old John Lee, for the murder of his employer, Miss Emma Keyse. He had been employed in service at The Glen in Babbacombe, near Torquay, for quite some time, and the evidence against him was weak and circumstantial and he swore his innocence. Curiously, Lee claimed he had a dream the night before his execution that he would not hang for the crime. In what has arguably become one of the most notorious of all British executions, Lee was placed on the gallows trap, the white cap pulled over his head, the noose around his neck, and the lever pushed, but the trap refused to open. Lee was removed and the trap was tested; it fell open easily. Closed again, Lee was put back on the drop and the lever pushed again, but the trap would still not open, despite Berry and the warders adding their weight by stamping on it with their heavy boots. Lee was removed from the chamber, the trap was again tested and it worked with no problems. Lee was brought back a third time, ready to meet his maker, but the trap failed yet again. The chaplain appealed to the Governor to intercede, but it was the medical officer who stepped forward and said to Berry, 'You may experiment as much as you like on a sack of flour, but you shall not experiment on this man any longer.'

Lee was granted a reprieve from death but had to serve a life sentence. He was released in December 1907. He made a tidy

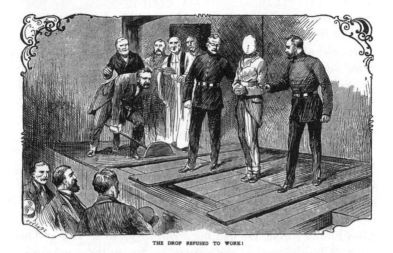

THE DROP REFUSED TO WORK!

living from his book *The Man They Could Not Hang*, and his story is told in the Fairport Convention album *'Babbacome' Lee* (1971). It is still debated to this day whether Lee did or did not kill Miss Keyse.

## WALES & WELSH BORDERS

*The Cuckoo Lane Explosion*
Forty-six-year-old mole catcher John Vaughan lived with his wife and eight-year-old-son on Cuckoo Lane, off Broad Haven Road in Haverfordwest, Pembrokeshire. In September 1913, Vaughan suspected his wife was having an affair and placed a dynamite cartridge and fuse under their bed, while his wife was out attending an evening service at Haverford Church. At about 3 a.m. the following day, Mr Vaughan slid out of bed, leaving his wife asleep and their child nearby, lit the fuse and made for the door. He had hardly reached the latch before the dynamite exploded. Vaughan was found dying near the front door and his wife and child were pulled dead from the rubble.

## The Llangybi Massacre

Farm labourer William Watkins lived with his wife and family in a remote cottage outside Llangybi, near Usk in Monmouthshire. On 16 July 1878, this idyllic home became the scene of a massacre. Mr Watkins was found in the garden, felled by a heavy fence post and subjected to multiple stab wounds, while his wife, Elizabeth, lay nearby; she too had been stabbed and her throat had been cut. Their house was on fire, but this was extinguished and three of their five children, Alice, aged four, Frederick, aged six, and Charlotte, aged eight, were found in the upstairs rooms (the other two daughters were not at home on this evening). Though their bodies had been burned, it was obvious their throats had been cut and horrific stab wounds were found on all of them.

The following day, 17 July, a suspicious character asked for a lift from the driver of a mail cart on the road near Newport, but the driver refused. He reported him to a constable and the man, a Spanish seaman named Joseph Garcia, aged twenty-one, was arrested. It transpired he had just been released from Usk County Gaol, having completed a nine-month stretch for burglary. His shirt was stained with blood and he carried with him two bundles. These were found to contain clothing that was later positively recognised by the two surviving Watkins sisters, and a pair of boots, which were recognised as belonging to Mr Watkins by the shoemaker that had made them.

Garcia spoke very little English but at his trial in October 1878, when found guilty of multiple murders, he murmured, 'I know nothing about it'. Garcia was executed on 18 November 1878 at Usk County Gaol.

## The Swansea Pier Tragedy

Every murder has tragedy associated with it, but this case, despite occurring well over 100 years ago, in 1885, remains tragic in the extreme. Thomas Nash, aged thirty-nine, was a widower with two children. Recently remarried, he had failed to tell his new wife about them. Nash managed to conceal the children by lodging them with a Mrs Goodwin in a suburb of Swansea for about three years. The eldest child was old enough to be in service and did not present too much of a problem, but, soon after the new marriage, Nash fell behind with his payments for the maintenance of his youngest child, six-year-old Mary Anne. Mrs Goodwin requested payment three times and Nash would always promise to settle up, but never did so. In exasperation, Mrs Goodwin took Mary Anne to Swansea Guildhall on 4 December 1885, where she knew Nash would be collecting his wages. There, she presented him with a bill and left without Mary Anne, stating that she could no longer keep her.

Nash set off walking with Mary Anne and strolled along the Swansea Extension Pier. He and his daughter had been noticed by a couple of men who had been watching some vessels come in. When they saw him leaving without the little girl they asked him what he had done with the child. Nash hesitated then said, 'She is on the top,' and soon after claimed, 'She is underneath.' The men did not like his answers and summoned a constable. Escorted back onto the pier, Nash explained, 'I put her upon the rail to take her on my back. She slipped down and the wind blew her off.'

Mary Anne's body was later discovered near the edge of the sea, having been left there by the receding tide – there was not a mark upon her. Nash was arrested and sent for trial for murder, where it was proved by the prosecution that it would have been impossible for the child to have slipped into the sea without striking some part of the pier structure on the way down. The wind direction was also proved to have more likely blown her onto the pier rather than off it. The jury retired but returned a short while later with a verdict of 'guilty' and Nash was sentenced to death. He was executed at Swansea Prison on 1 March 1886.

## Corpus Delicti
Chorus girl Maime Stuart, aged twenty-six, disappeared from the cottage she shared with her 'husband' George Shotton, overlooking Caswell Bay, on the Gower Peninsula in South

Wales, in December 1919. Curiously, Shotton disappeared at around the same time. Police investigations traced Shotton to another house, barely a mile away, where he was living with his wife, May, and their child. He admitted to knowing Maime but denied that they were married. Police were not satisfied and, acting on the belief that Shotton had killed Mamie, they searched the cottage and garden for clues as to Maime's whereabouts, as well as instigating a search across the surrounding countryside. Maime's description was also circulated to police forces across Britain and the story received high-profile coverage in the national press. But still nothing was found of Maime.

Shotton was brought to trial for bigamy, a charge he tried to deny by claiming another man had assumed his identity and married Maime on 25 March 1918. He then tripped himself up by admitting he had spent the night of that date in a hotel with Maime. Shotton was found guilty as charged and was sent down for eighteen months.

For years afterwards, reported sightings of Maime occasionally caught the attention of the media, until a sack containing human remains was discovered in a disused lead mine at Brandy Cove in November 1961. Removed to the Forensic Science Laboratory at Cardiff, Dr John Griffiths reassembled the skeleton. The body had been sawn into three sections; through the spine, the upper arms and thighs. Scraps of clothing found with the bones dated from the 1920s, the body was dated, through bone development, to a woman in her mid-twenties (there was no scientific method of identifying DNA at the time), and a wedding ring with a contemporary hallmark had also been found nearby. A portrait photograph of Maime was superimposed upon the skull, and it proved to be a match. But who had murdered her?

At the coroner's inquest held in December 1961, eighty-three-year-old Bill Symons, a retired postman, recalled seeing Shotton hauling a heavy sack into a van outside the cottage he had shared with Maime, at around the time of her disappearance. Symons confessed that he had not informed the police at the time, having dismissed any thoughts of the sack containing body parts as foolish. In the wake of the discovery and Symon's revelations, a police search began for Shotton. He was found sure enough, in a grave in Bristol, where he had died aged seventy-eight in 1958.

## Excuse Fingers

In appearance, Herbert Rowse Armstrong was a dapper, bespectacled, mild-mannered solicitor from Hay-on-Wye, on the border of England and Wales. He had seen action in France while serving as a Major during the First World War, and preferred to be addressed as Major Armstrong. However, his wife, Katharine, was a domineering woman and was known to denigrate her husband in public. The humiliation and unhappiness she caused festered in her husband's mind, and he showed little remorse when she died in 1921. Later that same year, Armstrong and rival Hay solicitor Oswald Martin were representing opposing parties in a property sale. A wrangle arose and Armstrong kept making excuses not to complete, but Martin was persistent in his requests for Armstrong to deal with the matter. Armstrong invited Martin over for tea at his home on 26 October, during which Armstrong passed him a scone saying, 'Excuse fingers'. When Martin got home he was violently ill. Martin's father-in-law was Hay chemist John Davies, who recalled that he had made several sales of arsenic to Major Armstrong, who claimed that he was purchasing the poison to kill dandelions. Suspicion was also aroused in Dr Hincks, who had attended Mrs Armstrong and now attended Martin and saw a similarity in the symptoms. Hincks contacted the Home Office and the matter was placed in the hands of Scotland Yard. Armstrong was arrested in December 1921, charged with the attempted murder of Oswald Martin.

When Armstrong's house was searched, a number of packets of arsenic were found, and, as a result, an exhumation was ordered for the body of Mrs Armstrong. Pathologist Bernard Spilsbury conducted the post-mortem and found her body was riddled with arsenic, and Armstrong was sent to trial for the murder of his wife. In court, however, Armstrong maintained that he was innocent. The evidence was circumstantial, and no one had actually seen him administer any poison. But the jury were convinced otherwise and Armstrong was sentenced to death. His execution was carried out by John Ellis at Gloucester Prison on 31 May 1922. It was reported that when he was asked by the prison governor if he had anything to say, Armstrong replied, 'I am innocent of the crime for which I am condemned to die'. It is believed that Armstrong is the only solicitor in the history of the United Kingdom to have been hanged for murder.

# LONDON

*Mrs Brownrigg*
Mrs Elizabeth Brownrigg earned her living from the private lying-in hospital she ran in Flower de Luce Court on Fetter Lane in London. However, her first priority was not to her patients but to her numerous children – and the staff she employed came last of all. They had to be cheap, so she employed orphaned girls for household duties. For some reason, Brownrigg sadistically tortured her staff. One unfortunate girl, named Mary Jones, was stripped naked and stretched out between two chairs and flogged until Brownrigg's arms gave out. Another girl, Mary Clifford, was also stripped naked, suspended by her bound hands from the ceiling and flogged over a period of hours; she was then forced to sleep on a filthy mat in the coal cellar. A concerned neighbour was moved to investigate and found yet another girl, Mary Mitchell, covered with ulcerated sores. The discovery was reported to the authorities and a warrant was issued for the arrest of Brownrigg, along with her husband and son. By the time the case came to court, Mary Clifford had died of the wounds that had been inflicted upon

her and the charge was upped to murder. Mrs Brownrigg was found guilty of murder, while her husband and son were found guilty of complicity in her beating of the girls and were given six months each. Mrs Brownrigg was executed before a

large crowd at Tyburn on 14 September 1767. She drew no sympathy but her body drew hundreds of people who came to see it when it was exhibited at Surgeon's Hall.

## The Ratcliffe Highway Murders

The Ratcliffe Highway was a rough part of the East End of London, which ran from East Smithfield to Shadwell High Street. About midnight on 7 December 1811, Timothy Marr, a twenty-four-year-old mercer who lived with his family on his premises at No. 29 Ratcliffe Highway, sent his servant girl, Margaret Jewell, out on an errand. After about twenty minutes the girl returned and rang the bell, but received no answer and no lights were on in the building. Margaret was clearly concerned when she could not get back in. Nightwatchman George Olney knew the Marrs and came over to enquire what was going on. He also tried knocking on the door and called out, but to no avail. Eventually Olney and a neighbour, John Murray, went to investigate and managed to enter the building. There, they discovered the bodies of the Marr family, horrifically beaten to death.

A hue and cry was raised and the Thames River Police were soon on the scene. A search of the house revealed a ship carpenter's maul, the iron head covered with fresh blood and a few hairs. Curiously, little or no money had been stolen – had the murderous robbers been disturbed or was there another reason for the annihilation of the Marrs? Posters appealed for information and a reward (to be paid on conviction of the perpetrator) was offered for relevant information.

Shortly after 11 p.m. on 19 December 1811, John Turner jumped from a window in the King's Arms public house in the neighbourhood of Old Gravel Lane, Ratcliffe Highway, shouting, 'They are murdering the people in the house!' Members of the public came running to the scene, as did members of the watch. The pub was entered and the landlord, fifty-six-year-old Jack Williamson, was found at the foot of the cellar stairs with a horrific blow to his head, his throat cut and an iron crowbar by his side. Mrs Elizabeth Williamson, aged sixty, and their servant, Bridget Harrington, were then found in the parlour; their skulls were smashed in and their throats cut, blood still issuing from the wounds. But the killers had got away again.

On Monday 23 December, an Irish sailor named Williams was apprehended on suspicion of being involved in the murders. Known to frequent the Williamson's pub he had been there on the night in question, and a sailor who shared his lodgings at the Pear Tree pub recalled that Williams had complained he was short of money, but when he was arrested he had been found in the possession of £1 and a considerable amount of silver. Williams claimed that he had obtained this money from pawning some of his clothes. Further investigations suggested the maul, now missing, but known to have been owned by Williams, may well have been the one used in the murderous attack on the Marrs.

The truth may never be known because Williams was found dead, hanged from his neck handkerchief in his cell before his

trial. His body was taken through the street on a cart with a full ceremonial escort. Arriving at a section of what was then New Road at St George's Turnpike, where Canon Street Road and Cable Street in St George-in-the-East crossed over each other, the body of Williams was unceremoniously hurled into a suicide's grave dug in the road, it was then pinned with a stake through the heart and the road filled in on top.

## The Murder of Lord Russell

When Lord William Russell found out some silverware had gone missing from his home at No. 14 Norfolk Street, London in May 1840, suspicion fell upon his valet, Francois Benjamin Courvoisier. Russell did not want to attract attention or scandal over the matter so he ordered Courvoisier to resign from the household. Rather than lose his position, Courvoisier decided to murder Russell while he slept, in order to conceal the matter. He also attempted to make it look as if there had been a break-in and robbery, but valuables found secreted in the wainscoting of Courvoisier's pantry only caused the finger of blame to level more against him. Tried and found guilty of the murder of his master, Courvoisier subsequently confessed to the crime and was executed outside Newgate Prison on 6 July 1840. The execution drew a massive crowd, estimated at 40,000; among them were two great authors, Charles Dickens and William Makepeace Thackeray, who would both write about their revulsion of the spectacle they saw that day.

## The First Wanted Poster with a
## Composite Picture of the Wanted Man

On 27 June 1881, sixty-four-year-old coin dealer Frederick Gold was attacked, robbed and thrown out of the carriage of the moving train he was travelling on between London and Brighton. His assailant was bloodstained and in disarray after the attack, and attracted concerned attention at the station where he alighted before he slipped away. A manhunt ensued, led by C.E. Howard Vincent, Director of the CID, who called upon the British press for their assistance. For the very first

time the description of
the wanted person was
accompanied by an
artist's impression, based
on the descriptions given
by witnesses. Published
in the *Daily Telegraph*, it
created enormous public
interest that resulted in
erroneous sightings of
the wanted man all over
the country. The man
turned out to be one
Percy Lefroy Mapleton,
who was traced through
detective work rather
than being identified

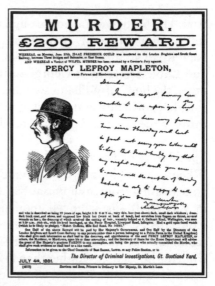

from his published image, but the police had found such
images were a valuable asset in raising the profile of their
investigation and are still in use to this day.

## The Murder of 'Breezy Bill'

As the nineteenth century drew to a close, a murder so indicative
of Victorian melodrama, fuelled by the age old motive of
jealousy, occurred on 16 December 1897. William 'Breezy Bill'
Terriss, one of the leading actors of his day, was stabbed to
death at his private entrance to the Adelphi Theatre in London
by Richard Archer Prince. Prince, known to acquaintances as
'Mad Archie', was a failed actor turned inveterate letter writer
who sent high-handed missives to theatrical managers or
fawning letters of commiseration or congratulations to royalty
or celebrities, depending on the occasion. He was thought
harmless enough by most.

Prince had a minor role in a run of *The Harbour Lights*, but
Terriss took offence to a comment Prince made about him
and had Prince dismissed. Terriss, however, sent small sums
of money to Prince, via the Actors' Benevolent Fund, and

continued to try to find him acting engagements. By the end of
1897, Prince was destitute and desperate for work but he had
become unemployable. In December 1897 Prince attempted to
get a complimentary ticket to the Vaudeville Theatre, which
adjoined the Adelphi; he was turned down and forcibly ejected.
Prince brooded on this event and a combination of jealousy of
Terriss's success and blaming Terriss for the rotten situation

THE LATE WILLIAM TERRISS

HOUSE WHERE PRISONER LIVED

M<sup>R</sup> TERRISS'S HOME

he was in, Prince stepped out of the shadows and carried out his revenge. Convicted of the murder but found insane, Prince spent the rest of his years at Broadmoor Criminal Lunatic Asylum, occasionally putting on concerts with the other inmates until his death there in 1936.

## The Flypaper Poisoner

Forty-year-old Frederick Seddon was a former insurance agent who had left the business to try his hand at real estate speculation. He was always looking for ways to make money and saw a great opportunity in forty-nine-year-old spinster Eliza Barrow, who was easily duped by the plausible Seddon. He persuaded her to sign over her considerable savings and stocks to him so that he could manage them for her, ensuring her that if she did she would be looked after for the rest of her life. Seddon soon moved her into to his family home and allowed her to live there 'rent free', but this was not a situation he was willing to put up with for too long. He sent his daughter to buy flypapers (containing arsenic) and very soon Miss Barrow was suffering from agonising stomach pains; she died a few days later on 14 September 1911. Fortunately for Seddon, the doctor that had attended her suspected no wrongdoing and issued a death certificate without seeing the body, claiming he could not attend in person due to the outbreak of an epidemic illness in the area at the time.

After Mrs Barrow's funeral her cousin, Frank Vonderahe, contacted Seddon to claim the residue of her estate, only to be informed that there was nothing left. Vonderahe was suspicious and went to the police to voice his worries, and Miss Barrow's corpse was exhumed. At the post-mortem, two gains of arsenic were detected in the body. Arrested and brought to trial, Seddon had Edward Marshall Hall leading his defence, who built a strong argument explaining that the presence of arsenic in her body had come from the medical preparation she had been taking, which contained the poison. Despite being advised against it by Marshall

Hall, Seddon insisted in giving evidence in his own defence. His arrogance and condescending attitude endeared him to no one, especially his ludicrous assertion that Miss Barrow may have drunk the water from the dishes of flypaper in her room. The jury returned a verdict of 'guilty' and when the learned judge asked if he had anything to say before he passed sentence, Seddon, a former Freemason, made a Masonic symbol and appealed to the judge, who he knew to also be a mason, to overturn the verdict. Judge Sir Thomas Townsend Bucknill rightly replied, 'It is not for me to harrow your feelings – try to make peace with your Maker. We both belong to the same Brotherhood, and though that can have no influence with me, this is painful beyond words to have to say what I am saying, but our Brotherhood does not encourage crime, it condemns it.'

Seddon was hanged at Pentonville Prison by John Ellis on 18 April 1912.

*True Story?*

Ronald True was the son of a well-to-do family and certainly cut a dash as a handsome young officer in the Royal Flying Corps during the First World War. But his behaviour was always considered rather odd, a situation not helped by his addiction to morphia, and he was discharged from service in 1916, after crashing three of his aircraft. His mental state continued to deteriorate; he left his family and lived off his allowance and a series of petty frauds and thefts. As time went on his behaviour became more eccentric, as did his absolute belief that there was a man impersonating him who was his mortal enemy. True had spent a night with twenty-five-year-old prostitute Olive Young (real name Gertrude Yates) at her flat on Finsborough Road, Earls Court, but she found him a frightening and disturbing client and did not return his calls requesting another meeting.

On 6 March 1922, Olive's cleaner passed True on his way out and he murmured to her, 'Do not disturb Miss Young. We were late last night and she is in a deep sleep,' before he left. When the maid went into the bathroom she discovered the dead body of Young. She had been badly battered, with a dressing gown cord tied around her neck and a towel pushed down her throat. True was traced and arrested the same night at the Hammersmith Palace. Tried at the Old Bailey, much discussion was given over to True's mental state; the jury believed that he was aware of what he was doing, that he knew it was a wrong thing to do and that he should face the full rigor of the law. True was found guilty of murder and sentenced to death. The Home Secretary granted him a reprieve and True was sent to Broadmoor Prison for the criminally insane, where he actively participated in the hospital drama productions along with Richard Prince, the murderer of William Terriss, who acted as conductor for the hospital band. True remained at Broadmoor until his death in 1951.

*Murder at the Savoy*

On 9 July 1923, Prince Ali Kamel Fahmy Bey, dapper international playboy and heir to a vast Egyptian fortune, and his strikingly beautiful European wife, Marie-Marguerite, were ensconced in their luxury suite at London's famous Savoy Hotel on the Strand. While in the exclusive restaurant, where etiquette was everything, they were heard to quarrel over an operation Madame Fahmy wished to have performed in Paris but for which her husband would only pay if she had it done in England. The leader of the small orchestra tried to diffuse the situation by asking if Madame would like a particular tune, to which she replied, 'I don't want any music ... My husband has threatened to kill me tonight.' With a polite bow and a withering smile the conductor departed, saying, 'I hope you will still be here tomorrow, Madame.'

Shortly after retiring to bed at 1.30 a.m., the Prince flung open their apartment door, launched himself into the corridor and said to a passing porter, 'Look what she has done to my face' – his cheek had apparently been slapped. The porter, the soul of discretion, simply acknowledged him and walked on. Before he reached the end of the corridor, however, he heard three gunshots in quick succession. Running back to the Fahmy's suite, the porter saw Madame Fahmy holding a smoking pistol; on the floor beneath her, with fatal head wounds, was her husband.

At the trial much was made of the known homosexual affairs of the Prince, his mistreatment of Marie-Marguerite, the dreadful mistake she had made of 'marrying an oriental' and, very carefully, it was stated in court that the Prince had demanded regular anal sex with her, to the extent she required the operation which had led to the argument at the dinner table.

Brilliantly defended by Edward Marshall Hall, his trump card was the pistol. Painting a picture of a white woman defending herself from the unnatural sexual proclivities of an eastern potentate, Marshall Hall argued that Marie-Marguerite had simply raised the gun to frighten her husband and her trembling hand on the hair trigger of the pistol had accidentally set it off. When this was demonstrated by Marshall Hall in court it swung the verdict – Madame Fahmy was found not guilty of murder, to the pleasure of the cheering crowd. The pressure exerted for the rapid fire of the 'hair trigger' of the Fahmy pistol caused bruising and swelling on Marshall Hall's index finger for about two weeks afterwards.

### Murder at London Zoo

Said Ali had been employed during the summer months at the Zoological Gardens on Regent's Park, where he trained and drove elephants so that children might ride on them. At the end of the season Ali would return home to India for the winter months, something he had done since he began his employment in 1922.

Sann Dwe Nari was a twenty-two-year-old Burmese mahout who came to Britain with another five men in charge of Pa Wa, the sacred Burmese white elephant. Dwe was asked if he would like to stay and work at the zoo until Ali returned, to which he agreed. The following June, Ali returned to his work and Dwe was sent to the sanatorium to look after, but not drive, the baby elephants, which resulted in Dwe losing the lucrative tips of the previous job.

Dwe was given accommodation above the Tapir House at the zoo, which Ali shared with him. Dwe was jealous of Ali and the pair did not get on well. Matters came to a head on 24 August 1928, when, fuelled by jealousy and the desire to rob his roommate, Dwe confronted Ali. The pair rowed and Ali was discovered dead in his bed, having been badly battered with a pickaxe. Dwe was found guilty of murder and sentenced to death. This was, however, commuted to penal servitude for life.

### The Cleft Chin Murder

US Army soldier Karl Gustav Hulten met eighteen-year-old Georgina Grayson (real name Elizabeth Jones) in a teashop on Hammersmith Broadway on 3 October 1944. The pair lived more for their fantasies than reality; she fantasized about being a stripper and he spun yarns about being an officer and having been a gangster back in Chicago. Over the following six days they lived out a reckless gangster and moll odyssey during which they stole an army truck and knocked down a girl on a county lane and stole her handbag. They picked up a hitchhiker, Hulten knocked her unconscious with an iron bar, half strangled her, robbed her and then dumped her body near a stream – fortunately, she survived.

Then there was taxi driver George Heath, a man with a cleft chin, who was shot dead by Hulten with an automatic pistol on 7 October. Hulten then drove off in the taxi, dumping the body by the road to Staines. The pair blew the proceeds of this murderous robbery at the White City dog track the following day. A description of the vehicle and the registration number, RD 8955, was circulated to all police stations and it was found on Fulham Palace Road; officers kept watch and Hulten was arrested when he returned to the vehicle. Jones was named by Hulten as his alibi and she was picked up the following day. Coming to her senses and realising the magnitude of what she had been involved in, she wrote her version of the events in a confession. During the six-day trial, the pair implicated each other. Both were found guilty and were sentenced to hang, but only Hulten went to the gallows at Pentonville on 8 March 1945, just five days after his twenty-third birthday. Jones had her sentenced commuted to imprisonment and was released on license in 1954. The 1990 film *Chicago Joe and the Showgirl* was based on the story.

### Love Me, Love Me Not

Ruth Ellis had worked her way around the London entertainment scene as nightclub hostess, nude model and even as an occasional film extra, such as her brief un-credited appearance in *Lady Godiva Rides Again* (1951). In 1953, Ellis became a nightclub manager in her own right; she lived the high life, with admirers as well as celebrity friends. She was introduced to racing driver David Blakely in 1953 and within weeks he had moved in with her, although he was engaged to another woman at the time. Their relationship was up and down. Ellis became pregnant but, feeling she could not commit to Blakely, had an abortion. Ellis and Blakely continued to see other people whilst continuing their relationship, despite it becoming more and more embittered. Ellis became pregnant again and this time Blakely offered to marry her, she accepted but later an argument erupted between the pair and Blakely punched Ellis hard in the stomach and she lost the baby.

On Easter Sunday, 10 April 1955, Ellis went in search of Blakely. She had a fair idea he would be at a pub called The Magdala Tavern in South Park Hill, Hampstead. He left there at about 9.30 p.m. and Ruth was waiting outside, but he ignored her when she said 'Hello David'. As he kept on walking, she shouted 'David!' and as he stopped and searched for the keys to his car Ellis produced a .38 Smith and Wesson revolver from her handbag and opened fire on Blakely. The first shot missed and he ran. The second hit him and he collapsed onto the pavement. Ellis then walked over, stood directly over him and fired a further three shots into his body. As Ellis stood transfixed over the body she was arrested by off-duty policeman Alan Thompson. Tried at Court No. 1 at the Old Bailey, the case drew national and international media interest. The jury took just fourteen minutes to return a verdict of 'guilty'. Executed at Holloway Prison by Albert Pierrepoint on 13 July 1955, Ruth Ellis, aged twenty-eight, was the last woman to be hanged in Great Britain.

## SCOTLAND

### Burke and Hare

The most notorious bodysnatchers of all time were William Burke and William Hare, who sold corpses to Dr Robert Knox, a private anatomy lecturer whose students were drawn from the Edinburgh Medical College. They did not, however, dig up the bodies they sold – their victims were murdered. The first

*Bodysnatchers Burke and Hare.*

body to be handed over to Dr Knox came when a tenant died, who owed rent at the lodging house kept by Hare's wife at Tanner's Close in the West Port area of Edinburgh. To recoup their losses they sold his body to Knox. Discovering that this was easy money, Burke and Hare set about 'helping' the sick to shuffle off this mortal coil by suffocating them, before taking the fresh bodies to the surgeon.

Twelve months later and the pair had built up quite a business, but ultimately they were detected in their dark business and brought to trial. Hare was offered immunity from prosecution if he confessed and testified against Burke; this he did, saving his own neck but sending Burke to the gallows. Burke was executed on 28 January 1829 and ironically, after execution, his body was publicly dissected at the Medical College. His skeleton is still on display at the University of Edinburgh's Anatomical Museum. The term 'Burking' soon became common parlance for bodysnatching.

### Dr Pritchard
Dr Edward William Pritchard was an English doctor working in Glasgow when his mother-in-law died, aged seventy, in February 1865. His wife died a month later and two deaths in such close succession did not pass without drawing some

suspicion. Dr Paterson, who had helped to treat both Pritchard's mother and wife, would not sign their death certificates – so Pritchard wrote them himself. Paterson, however, did not directly report his concerns to the authorities either; action was only set in motion after an anonymous letter was received by the Procurator Fiscal. The corpses of both women were exhumed and the poison antimony was found in both bodies. Pritchard was arrested and brought to trial. The case drew a great deal of interest from both the press and the public. Much of the evidence given during the five-day trial came from

*Dr William Pritchard.*

servants in the Pritchard household. Pritchard was revealed as a philanderer who had had extra-marital relations with more than one of his servants. Their testimony highlighted the links between Mrs Pritchard's bouts of illness and her consuming food that the doctor had come in contact with. Convicted of murder, Pritchard was executed by William Calcraft in front of a crowd of thousands at the Saltmarket end of Glasgow Green on 28 July 1865.

## The Sandyford Murder Case

Jess M'Pherson was found murdered in July 1862 at No. 17 Sandyford Place in Glasgow, where she was employed as staff. She had been hacked to death with a cleaver in a vicious attack, during which she suffered over forty wounds to her body. Her body was found by her employer, eighty-seven-year-old James Fleming, and his son John in her room after they had gone searching for her. There were a few clues; some plated cutlery was found missing, as was one of Jess's dresses, and, despite being recently cleaned, bloodstains were found in the kitchen and in the cellar.

The police surgeon was of the opinion that the wounds inflicted upon Jess showed a 'light degree of strength that would indicate a woman or weak man'. Suspicion initially fell on old James Fleming and he was arrested. However, a pawnbroker came forward and gave information that a plate matching the description of the one stolen from Jess's room had been pawned by a woman, who had given a false name, and suspicion turned towards Jessie M'Lachlan, a young woman who had also been a servant for Fleming. The description of the woman taking the plate to the pawnbroker was a good match for M'Lachlan but she doggedly maintained her innocence throughout her trial, accusing James Fleming instead. She suggested that he had lashed out in a fit of anger when Jess had rebuffed him after he had been drunkenly 'trying to use liberties with her'. The jury remained unconvinced and found M'Lachlan guilty after retiring for just fifteen minutes and she was sentenced to death.

Such was the public outcry at the outcome of the trial that a 50,000 signature petition was presented, requesting further enquiries be made before the execution was carried out. A commission was convened to look at the case again and although they did not acquit M'Lachlan, her sentenced was commuted to penal servitude for life. Jessie was released from Perth Prison in 1877, went to America, remarried and died in obscurity in 1899.

*Jessie M'Lachlan.*

## Eugène Marie Chantrelle

Eugène Marie Chantrelle was a French-born school teacher who obtained a position at Newington Abbey Private School in Edinburgh. While there he formed an inappropriate relationship with one of his pupils, Elizabeth Cullen Dyer, and to avoid a scandal when she became pregnant, he married her when she turned sixteen. The child was born two months later and another three children followed in close succession. Chantrelle resented having to marry and continued to have relationships with other women, and he frequently got drunk and was abusive towards his wife. During such outbursts he had been heard to threaten to kill her with poison. Chantrelle soon got into financial difficulties and ominously took out an accidental death insurance policy on his wife's life for £1,000 in 1877. Elizabeth Chantrelle became ill on New Year's Day 1878 and she was removed, unconscious, to the Royal Infirmary, where she died later that same day. Chantrelle tried to suggest she had suffered coal gas poisoning from a leaking gas pipe in their house. The post-mortem revealed neither gas nor narcotic poisoning, but an examination of a vomit stain on her nightdress did show traces of opium. Chantrelle was arrested and put on trial for murder. The trial lasted four days and it was proved he had opium in his possession. Chantrelle argued that the stains on his wife's nightdress had been put there to incriminate him but he could not suggest by whom. The evidence against him was circumstantial but the jury were convinced and he was found guilty of murder. He was given the death sentence, and Eugène Marie Chantrelle was hanged at Calton Jail on 31 May 1878. He swore his innocence to the end.

## The Beast of Birkenshaw

Peter Manuel was born in New York in 1927 to Scottish parents, who returned to Scotland when Peter was still just a young lad. Growing up in Birkenshaw, Lanarkshire, Peter had spells in approved schools and borstals and by the mid-1950s he had already accrued a number of prosecutions and prison sentences for sexual attacks and rape. Between 1956 and his arrest in January 1958 he turned to murder; he was prosecuted on eight counts but was suspected of killing as many as eighteen. There were sexually motivated killings, whereby Manuel would assault, rape and then kill his victims, but there was also the case of a murdered taxi driver and the killing of two family groups – Marion Watt, forty-five, her daughter Vivienne, sixteen, and Marion's sister, Margaret Brown, forty-one; and the Smart family, Peter, forty-five, Doris, forty-two, and Michael Smart, aged ten, who Manuel killed before living in their house for nearly a week, surviving off the family's leftover food. He was finally caught when he paid for drinks with a banknote known to have been stolen from the Smart family home.

Arrested and brought into police custody Manuel initially denied everything, he then confessed to a few murders, before he hen upped the number to twelve after he was confronted by his mother at the police station where he was being held. Tried at Glasgow High Court, Manuel was found guilty of murder on seven of the eight counts brought against him in court. Manuel was hanged at Barlinnie Prison in Glasgow on 11 July 1958. Shortly before his execution he confessed to the murders he had been convicted of, as well as a few more that had not been previously attributed to him. Manuel's last words are reported to have been, 'Turn up the radio, and I'll go quietly.'

## 2

# POISONERS – MASTERS
# OF THE SILENT KILLER

## MARY BLANDY

Mary Blandy became infamous in the mid-eighteenth century. An unusual murderer in her day, she was both educated and middle class; her father, Francis Blandy, was a notary and the town clerk at Henley-on-Thames. Blandy had become infatuated with Captain William Henry Cranstoun and they planned to marry but the problem was that Cranstoun was already married to another woman, who he had a child with in Scotland; he denied the validity of the marriage and made a number of trips north of the border, allegedly to sort the matter out. Mary's father was not convinced by Cranstoun, however, and believed he was deliberately procrastinating and did not hide his disapproval of the proposed marriage.

In court, Mary claimed that Cranstoun had sent her 'love potions' and asked her to place them in her father's food, to make him approve of their relationship. Mary did this, but the love potion was in fact arsenic. Her father became progressively ill over a number of months, before dying in August 1751. When Cranstoun heard of Mary's arrest he fled to France, where he died in 1752. Mary was tried at the Oxford Assizes and, despite her impassioned protestations, was found guilty of murder and was hanged in public on 6 April 1752. Her last request, born from the fear that young

MISS BLANDY *at the place of Execution near Oxford, attended by the Rev.ᵈ Mr. Swinton*

men in the crowd at her execution might look up her skirt, was, 'For the sake of decency, gentlemen, don't hang me high.'

## THE RUGELEY POISONER

Dr William Palmer, known in the annals of crime as 'The Rugeley Poisoner', worked from his surgery in his home town of Rugeley in Staffordshire. Palmer earned a reasonable living but not enough to support his gambling habit; he was often in debt and the situation became more serious as the years went by. A number of suspicious deaths occurred around Palmer, including a work colleague, his mother-in-law, five of his children and his wife, who he had insured for the considerable sum of £13,000. He also insured his wife's brother but he died too soon after the policy was taken out and the insurance company refused to pay. Child mortality and early deaths were accepted features of life in the nineteenth century and epidemic diseases were rife at the time, so these deaths did not attract particular suspicion. It was only after Palmer attended the Shrewsbury Handicap Stakes in November 1855 that suspicion fell upon him. Palmer lost heavily but his friend John Cook, who had accompanied him to the races, had done very well. A few days later Cook fell ill and died. At the ensuing inquest the jury returned a verdict of 'wilful murder'. Suspicions of foul play were aroused when Palmer attempted

*Dr William Palmer.*

to bribe several people involved with the coroner's inquest and with the discovery that Palmer had purchased strychnine shortly before Cook's death, Palmer was arrested. The bodies of Palmer's wife and her brother were exhumed and re-examined, but the findings were inconclusive. It was considered that Palmer would not receive an unbiased jury if tried in Staffordshire, and so he was tried at the Old Bailey. Found guilty of the murder of John Cook he was returned to Stafford Prison for execution. Palmer was hanged by George Smith in front of a crowd of 30,000 on 14 June 1856. As he stepped onto the gallows, he is said to have looked at the trapdoor and exclaimed, 'Are you sure it's safe?' His mother always believed her son innocent and after his execution commented, 'They have hanged my saintly Billy'.

## THE WIMBLEDON POISONER

Dr George Henry Lamson was an intelligent and adventurous young man who, after qualifying in 1874, had a promising career as a doctor ahead of him, but his addiction to morphine lost him his practice and consequently caused financial difficulties to the extent he lived by passing false cheques. If his young, disabled nephew, Percy John, was to die, Lamson would inherit over £700 through his wife's interest. Lamson began poisoning his nephew during a family holiday and continued when the boy returned to Blenheim Special School at Wimbledon. After a visit from his uncle in December 1881, when

*Dr George Lamson.*

Lamson gave the lad a slice of Dundee cake, Percy died. An alkaloid poison was detected in the boy's stomach during the post-mortem, and a raisin removed from the stomach was tested and found to contain aconite. Lamson was soon under arrest and at his trial, which lasted for six days, the jury ultimately had no doubt of his guilt and passed the guilty verdict after just thirty minutes. Lamson was executed at Wandsworth Prison by William Marwood on 28 April 1882.

WILLIAM MARWOOD FROM THE WAX MODEL IN MADAME TUSSAUDS

## MARY ANN COTTON

Mary Ann Cotton remains Britain's most prolific murderess. Born in Low Moorsley, County Durham in 1832, she moved with her family to Murton when she was eight. When she reached maturity she first worked as a nurse in the home of Edward Potter then returned to her family home, where she trained as a dress maker. It is difficult to ascertain exactly when she started poisoning her nearest and dearest but over the next twenty years she got through three husbands, her own mother, Joseph Nattras (her lover), Frederick Cotton, her fourth 'husband' (the marriage was bigamous), his sister, and the children from these various relationships. Every single one of her victims was insured, they all died of stomach disorders, and Mary was the beneficiary. It is thought Cotton could well have been responsible for as many as twenty-one deaths. She was finally exposed when her son Charles died; she went first to the insurance office, not to a doctor, and parish official Thomas Riley, who knew the family, raised his concerns

with the local doctor, persuading him to hold off signing the death certificate while the circumstances of the death were investigated further. The press soon picked up on the case and the trail of death Cotton had left behind her. The doctor who attended Charles had kept some samples from the boy and these tested positive for arsenic. Charles was exhumed and arsenic was also found in his body during the post-mortem.

At her trial, Cotton's defence argued the arsenic found in the boy's body had been inhaled from a dye that had been used in wallpaper in the Cotton home. The jury retired for ninety minutes and returned a verdict of 'guilty' against Mary Ann Cotton; she was sentenced to death and executed by William Calcraft at Durham County Gaol on 24 March 1873.

## THE BOROUGH POISONER

George Chapman was born Severin Klosowski in Nargornak, Poland, in 1865. While in Poland he was apprenticed to a surgeon before he moved to London in the 1880s. He worked as a hairdresser's assistant before taking up a similar position in a shop on the corner of Whitechapel High Street and George Yard. In 1889, he met Lucy Baderski at the Polish Club in Clerkenwell and the pair married in a whirlwind romance of just five weeks. Chapman proved to be a vicious husband and was seen using violence against Lucy on more than one occasion. The pair separated a number of times, until the relationship finally ended in 1892.

He met Annie Chapman (not to be confused with the victim of Jack the Ripper) in late 1893, and the pair lived together as man and wife. He took her surname and was known from then on as George Chapman. In 1896 he met the newly separated Mary Spink, ended his relationship with Chapman and went off with Spink to Hastings, where he leased a barber shop. While here he was also known to beat Mary. In September 1897 the pair returned to London and it was then that Mary Spink became violently ill with stomach pains and nausea; her condition became worse and she died in December, the cause of death was recorded as consumption.

In March 1899, Chapman met Elizabeth Taylor and the pair married. She died in February 1901, her symptoms similar to those suffered by Spink. The cause of her death, however, was recorded as 'internal obstruction and exhaustion'. Chapman then hooked up with Maude Marsh and entered into another illegal marriage with her in October 1899. In 1902, the couple took over The Crown public house on Borough High Street, but he soon tired of her and beat her, and it was not long before she too fell ill and died in October if that year.

The doctor was suspicious and he refused to issue a death certificate. A post-mortem was carried out that showed traces of the poison antimony. Chapman was arrested by Inspector Godley and the bodies of Chapman's other two deceased 'wives' were exhumed. Post-mortems were carried out and each of them was found to contain antimony.

The amorous adventures and poisonous murders committed by Chapman caught the imagination of both the press and the public. Tried and found guilty at the Old Bailey, Chapman was only convicted of the murder of Maud Marsh and hanged by William Billington at Wandsworth on 7 April 1903.

It was recorded at the time of Chapman's conviction that the then retired Chief Inspector Frederick Abberline, who had led the Whitechapel Murders investigation in 1888, said to his old comrade, Inspector Godley, 'You've got Jack the Ripper at last'. Sadly, most of Abberline's conclusions about Chapman as the Ripper, which were also published at the time, do not withstand closer scrutiny.

## THE BOVINGDON BUG

Graham Frederick Young was a strange lad. On the surface he appeared neat and clean, intelligent and well behaved, but behind the façade he was obsessed with Hitler, Nazism, black magic, poison and death. While he was still at school he attempted to poison his father and stepmother, his sister and even a school friend. This disturbed young man was committed to Broadmoor in July 1962. Young was released to a Government Training Centre in Slough upon his release in 1971, where he was soon up to his old tricks and poisoned, but failed to kill, storekeeper Trevor Sparkes. It was not proved that Young was responsible, however, and so no formal action was taken against him. Young managed to get a job at John Harland Ltd in Bovingdon, where he was to work as a storekeeper. Shortly after he arrived several members of staff were suddenly taken ill with a mystery illness that was soon dubbed 'The Bovingdon Bug'. Two of them, storeroom manager Bob Egle, and Fred Biggs, both died suffering from the 'Bug' and a more formal investigation revealed that both men and all the other staff that had been stricken had drunk tea or coffee made by Young. His background was investigated and Young was arrested. When his clothes were searched, police found a lethal dose of thallium in his pocket. Tried at St Albans in July 1972, Young received a life sentence for murder. He died of a heart attack whilst at Parkhurst Prison in August 1990.

## 3

# DISMEMBERMENT AND TRUNKS

## THE EDGEWARE ROAD MURDERER

James Greenacre got through wives at a rate of knots. He first got married when he was nineteen, to the daughter of a Woolwich innkeeper, but she died suddenly. Greenacre married again, to the daughter of a Romford landowner, but then she too died, 'of brain fever'. Fifteen months after the death of his second wife, Greenacre married a Miss Simmonds of Bermondsey. She bore him seven children but only two of them lived to maturity, then she also died.

Greenacre met his next prospective wife, Hannah Brown, via a newspaper advertisement. Hannah had been in the service of Lord Wodehouse at Kimberley Hall for about four years. Greenacre courted Brown; he soon proposed marriage and they became lovers. Greenacre continued to live and conduct his business in London, visiting Hannah in Norfolk for their liaisons. He also maintained a number of mistresses but became particularly smitten with a pretty younger woman named Sarah Gale. Greenacre was determined to forsake all others and start a new life with Gale, and was ready to break off his engagement to Hannah when she informed him she was pregnant and she was going to come down to London, in full anticipation of him making good his promise of marriage. Fearful that this would ruin his prospects with Miss Gale, Greenacre induced Hannah to come to his rooms on 24 December 1836.

What Greenacre planned to do next is unclear, but shortly after Hannah's arrival he killed her with a blow over the head from a silk roller. Greenacre then set about the grim task of disposing of the body. He decided not to try to move the whole unwieldy body at once – that would attract too much attention. Instead, Greenacre crudely dismembered her using a knife and an ordinary carpenter's saw then, under cover of darkness, dumped the body parts around London. The trunk of the body was found on Edgware Road, the legs on Coal Harbour Lane and, eventually, the head turned up after jamming a lock gate at Stepney! Greenacre was soon traced

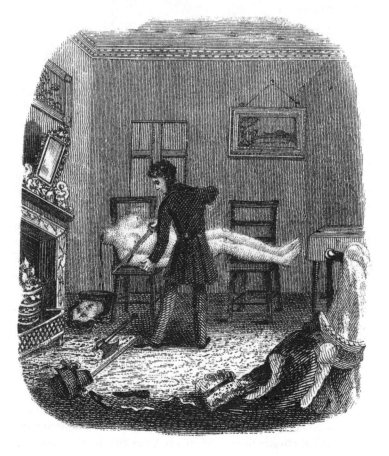

and when his apartments were searched, rags were found that corresponded with the rags the body parts were wrapped in. At Greenacre's trial the jury only took fifteen minutes to return a guilty verdict against him.

The case attracted massive national attention and his execution outside Newgate Prison on 2 May 1837 drew huge crowds. William Calcraft, the executioner, did his duty and then, biting into a very fine pie, proclaimed this repast was so good, filled with generous chunks of meat, that it should be known hence forward as a Greenacre, a morbid name which stuck for many years afterwards.

## THE TABERNACLE STREET HORROR

On 21 June 1851, the first of a number of body parts were found at a variety of locations around Norwich, Norfolk. During the following four weeks the police collected two hands, two feet, a thigh bone, lower leg bones, parts of a pelvis, some vertebrae and a grisly selection of flesh, strips of skin and muscle. The portions of flesh were preserved in wine and examined, along with the bones, by a team of local surgeons who concluded that the remains were those of an adult female. Their opinion of her age was pronounced as being about twenty-five years, yet there was a distinct absence of anyone answering the description being missing from the locale. Eventually, they concluded that it was a prank pulled by local medical students and the matter fell from public interest. That is until William Sheward, aged fifty-seven, walked into the suburban police station on Carter Street, Walworth in South London on 1 January 1869.

Sheward could no longer live with the guilt of murdering his wife Martha, and, having failed to take his own life, handed himself over to the police. He confessed that he had killed her by slashing her throat with his razor during an argument at their home on Tabernacle Street, Norwich. Over the next few days he had disposed of her body by dismembering it and distributing the parts around Norwich. Martha was not instantly missed; her closest family were in Wymondham and she was much older – fifty-four – than the age ascribed to the body parts by the surgeons. For years Sheward managed to fend off her family's enquiries of her whereabouts by claiming that she had run off to London and that he had not seen or heard from her in years. Sheward was returned to Norwich and tried before the Norfolk Lent Assizes in March 1869, where he was found guilty and sentenced to death. He was executed by William Calcraft within the walls of Norwich City Gaol on 20 April 1869.

## THE BUSINESSMAN, THE CHORUS GIRL AND HIS MISTRESS

Henry Wainwright was to all extents and purposes an upstanding Victorian family man, but he in fact had another family living between his home and his brush-making warehouse on the Whitechapel Road, London. Wainwright was quite cautious and lived out his other life with Harriet Lane, and their two children, under the false identities of Mr and Mrs King. Things started to go wrong when Wainwright's lifestyle outweighed his income; he got into financial difficulties and he had to cut Harriet's allowance, before moving her to cheaper accommodation and sending the children to stay with friends. Harriet went to Wainwright's warehouse to complain and during their altercation, Wainwright shot Harriet. He then hid her body in a drain on the premises.

When bankruptcy forced Wainwright out of his warehouse he was faced with the dilemma of removing the body. On 11 September 1875, his brother, Thomas, assisted him in dismembering the body, before hiding the parts in packages. Employee Alfred Stokes became suspicious about the packages, raised the alarm and summoned the police to pursue the hansom cab carrying Wainwright and the packages. When the cab stopped at its destination on Borough High Street,

THE WHITECHAPEL TRAGEDY

the police moved in and found Wainwright with Violet Dash, a Pavilion chorus girl he had picked up and given a lift along the way, and the body parts of Harriet Lane wrapped in two parcels of American cloth. After Violet Dash was acquitted of any involvement, Wainwright and his brother were left to stand trial. Thomas was given seven years' hard labour for his complicity but Henry Wainwright was found guilty of murder and sentenced to death. As he approached the Newgate gallows on 21 December 1885, he called to those assembled to observe, 'Come to see a man die have you, you curs?'

## WHEN EMPLOYING SERVANTS...

Kate Webster was an Irish conwoman working as a cook and general servant to widow Mrs Julia Martha Thomas at No. 2,

Mayfield Park Villas on Park Road in Richmond, in January 1879. Thomas was known for her reputation for being a tartar towards her servants and  found it difficult to retain staff because of this. After greatly increasing her workload and finding fault with her work, Mrs Thomas gave notice to Webster. On the Sunday before she was to leave, Webster and Thomas argued. From the early hours of the following morning, the sounds of washing and brushing were heard coming from the villa. The washing was hung out to dry and all seemed normal except for an unusual smell emanating from the kitchen.

On 5 March 1879, a trunk full of human flesh washed up in the Thames and a human foot was found in a dung hill. When Webster started selling Mrs Thomas's clothes, people began to question where Mrs Thomas was. Police investigations found the villa abounded with clues. Mrs Thomas had been cut up, boiled and burnt on the kitchen and copper grates. Webster fled to Ireland but was traced, tried, found guilty and executed on 29 July 1897. Anyone who employed staff would have shuddered when reading about this case, but one can only wonder how those who had bought the gallipots of meat dripping hawked by Webster felt when they heard how she had dealt with her mistress.

## THE CHARLOTTE STREET BUTCHER

During the air raid on London on 31 October 1917, thirty-one-year-old Émillienne Gérard fled for shelter at the home of her lover, Belgian butcher Louis Voisin, aged fifty, on Charlotte Street. Discovering that another woman named Berthe Roche, thirty-eight, had become Voisin's live-in lover, a violent exchange occurred between the pair. What actually happened next is unclear but it seems Roche inflicted serious wounds upon Gérard. The *coup de grâce*, however, was probably delivered by Voisin himself, when he attempted to intervene. It then fell to Voisin to use his skills as a butcher to dismember Gérard's body and dispose of it. The first of the body parts to be discovered, her torso and arms to be precise, were wrapped up in a sheet, put into a meat sack and dumped in the gardens of Regent Square; nearby, the legs were found in a parcel on which the words 'Blodie Belgium' were scrawled, in an attempt to confuse the police. The sheet the body had been wrapped in carried a laundry mark that led to Roche and ultimately to Voisin and his coal cellar on Charlotte Street, where bloodstains were discovered. It was here that the head and hands of Gérard were found hidden in a barrel of sawdust. Voisin was found guilty of murder and was executed by John Ellis at Pentonville Prison on 2 March 1918. Roche was acquitted of murder but was convicted as an accessory and was sent down for seven years. Shortly after her committal to prison, Roche was found insane and was removed to an asylum, where she died in 1919.

## THE CHARING CROSS TRUNK MURDER

On 6 May 1927, a dress trunk was deposited at the cloakroom at Charing Cross Station, London. Four days later, on 10 May, a foul smell emitted from the trunk and attracted the attention of cloakroom clerk, Albert Glass. He forced the trunk open and found five brown paper parcels tied with string, each containing dismembered human body parts.

The remains were sent to pathologist Bernard Spilsbury for examination, who concluded that all of the parts were from the same woman, aged about thirty-five. The only clues to the identity of the victim were a pair of knickers bearing a tab marked 'P. HOLT' and a number of laundry marks on other items of clothing. These were traced to a Mrs Holt, who was alive and well in Chelsea, but there was a chance that these had been stolen by a member of her house staff in the last two years. All staff members were accounted for, except a certain Mrs Rolls. The investigating officers asked if Mrs Holt would be kind enough to identify the remains and she confirmed the body was that of her former servant Rolls.

Investigations revealed that the woman known as Mrs Rolls was in fact Minnie Alice Bonati, who had been working as a prostitute in London. Meanwhile, investigations had also been made into the trunk, which was eventually recognised by the shop owner who had sold it. He gave a good description of the purchaser – a man, aged about thirty-five, 5ft 8-10in tall, with a dark complexion, dark hair, sharp features and military bearing. A cabby then came forward who remembered picking up a man from Rochester Row who answered the description, and recalled helping him load a heavy trunk and driving him to Charing Cross Station. Police located the exact house on Rochester Row and went to interview the tenant, thirty-six-year-old clerk John Robinson.

Although he could no longer be found at that address, Robinson was traced and questioned but denied all knowledge of the crime; the cab driver also failed to pick him out in a line-up. The police did not give up, however, and when they were searching Robinson's offices they found a bloodstained match stuck in the wicker of his wastepaper basket. Robinson was pressed for answers and eventually confessed. He claimed he had been accosted by Bonati as he visited the post office at Victoria, and she had gone with him to his offices where she demanded money for sex. When he refused she became violent, he pushed her away and she fell and hit her head on the coal scuttle. Robinson claimed he had fled, anticipating she would leave when she came round, but when he returned she was still lying there – she was dead. At his trial, Robinson repeated his story but always swore he had not murdered Bonati. Spilsbury's evidence countered that the bruises he found upon her chest were consistent with someone holding her down, possibly strangling her. Robinson was found guilty of murder and hanged by Robert Baxter at Pentonville Prison on 12 August 1927.

## THE BRIGHTON TRUNK MURDERS

A horrible discovery was made at Brighton railway station on 17 June 1934, when the smell from an unclaimed plywood trunk resulted in it being opened. It was found to contain the dismembered torso of a woman. A police alert also led to the

SCENE IN THE BRIGHTON CLOAK ROOM

POLICE OFFICERS FORCED OPEN THE TRUNK

discovery of a pair of legs in a suitcase at King's Cross but the head and arms were never found. The body parts were sent for post-mortem examination by Home Office pathologist Bernard Spilsbury, who confirmed that the body parts came from the same woman, who he estimated to be about twenty-five years old and five months pregnant. The victim, dubbed 'The Girl with the Pretty Feet' because her feet were considered to be the fine feet of a dancer, remains unidentified and her killer was never traced.

Although unrelated, another grim discovery was made less than a month later on 15 July 1934, when the body of missing waitress and part-time prostitute Violet Kaye was discovered in a trunk at the lodgings of her lover Toni Mancini (real name Cecil Lois England). The post-mortem examination revealed her skull had been fractured. Mancini claimed he had returned home to the lodgings he had shared with Kaye at Park Crescent, Brighton to find her lying dead and bloody on the bed. He did not think the police would believe his story because he already had a criminal record, so he hid the body in a trunk; he even moved the trunk with him to his new lodgings, where he kept it at the foot of his bed. Mancini was fortunate to have his defence argued by Norman Birkett, one of the best barristers of his day. Birkett emphasised the shadowy and vulnerable practice of prostitution and planted the seed of doubt in the minds of the jury. Mancini was found not guilty. Shortly before his death in 1976, Mancini confessed to a *News of the World* reporter that Kaye had died as a result of him throwing a hammer, which they used to break coal for the fire, at her during an argument.

## BUCK RUXTON

Bombay-born Lancaster general practitioner Dr Buck Ruxton (born Bikhtyar Rustomji Ratanji Hakim) had a tempestuous marriage, and he and his wife, Isabella, were often heard arguing at their house on Dalston Square. On September 1935,

Ruxton accused Isabella of having an affair with a clerk from Lancaster Town Hall. Shortly afterwards, Ruxton claimed that both Isabella and Mary Jane Rogerson, the family nursemaid, were away on holiday in Edinburgh. Over the ensuing days, his two cleaning ladies, Mrs Curwen and Mrs Smith, along with a Mrs Hampshire, who Ruxton had employed to clean his house in preparation for the decorators, all noticed unusual stains around the house, most notably in the bath and on the carpets. Mrs Hampshire recalled that as she washed them 'the water that came off was like blood'. He also gave her a stained suit he suggested she could get cleaned for her husband, a suit which Ruxton tried to claw back the following day, claiming 'it was undignified for a man to wear another man's suit'. Then there was the unpleasant smell, which Ruxton attempted to cover up by sending Mrs Curwen to buy eau-de-Cologne and a syringe, in order for him to spray the house.

On 29 September 1935, the dismembered remains of two bodies were spotted by a holidaymaker under the bridge crossing Gardenholm Linn, a tributary of the Annan River near Moffat in Scotland. When recovered and examined, it was found that all the usual identifying characteristics had been removed from both bodies. However, a copy of the *Sunday Graphic*, with a 'slip copy' of local news for distribution in the Lancaster and Morecambe area, was found wrapped around one of the body parts, which led the Scottish police to contact Lancaster Borough Police.

On 9 October Mary Rogerson's mother reported her daughter missing; the following day Ruxton asked police to make 'discreet inquiries' into the disappearance of his wife. Items of clothing found with the bodies were traced to the Ruxton household, and Ruxton was charged with the murder of both his nursemaid and his wife a few days later. The forensics team, which included Professor John Glaister and Professor Sydney Smith, pieced together what was left of the bodies. Innovative forensic techniques were also used to identify them, notably large photographic prints were superimposed over the X-rays of the skulls and found to match. Casts of the feet of the remains were also found to fit the shoes of the missing women. Blood was also detected on the bath in the Ruxton house and under the floorboards, where the body parts had been hidden until Ruxton had a chance to remove and dump them.

Tried before Manchester Assizes in March 1936, Ruxton was found guilty of the murders. He was hanged at Strangeways Prison on 12 May 1936 by Thomas Pierrepoint, assisted by Robert Wilson. After his execution, his simple, signed confession was published: 'I killed Mrs Ruxton in a fit of temper because I thought she had been with a man. I was mad at the time. Mary Rogerson was present at the time. I had to kill her.'

# 4

# INFAMOUS MURDERS

## THE RED BARN MURDER

William Corder was the son of a prosperous farmer from Polstead in Suffolk. In 1826, he began a relationship with Maria Marten, who was no shrinking violet, having had more than one lover and at least one illegitimate child before meeting Corder. In 1827 she gave birth to a son in the rooms she shared with Corder at Sudbury. This child apparently died soon after Maria's return to Polstead and was buried, his remains undiscovered, somewhere in the village. On 18 May 1827, Corder told Maria to make discreet preparations to travel to Ipswich, where they would be married. She was to meet him in the evening at the 'Red Barn' disguised as a man and they would make their elopement.

Maria made her way to the barn and was never seen alive again. Corder reappeared in Polstead a few days later, stating that he had left Maria at Ipswich. He then departed to London, where he began advertising for a wife and soon set up a school with Mary Moore, his new bride, in Brentford. In the meantime, Maria's mother dreamt her daughter was dead and buried under the dirt floor of the Red Barn. Persuading her mole-catcher husband to investigate, old Mr Marten found his wife's dream proved horribly true and the body of Maria was unearthed on 19 April 1828 – she had been shot and apparently stabbed. Corder was brought back for trial but he claimed that

THE RED BARN AT POLSTEAD.

Maria had shot herself and vehemently denied stabbing her. The witnesses and evidence, however, piled up against him and he was found guilty and sentenced to death.

Bury St Edmunds' Gaol Governor, John Orridge, implored Corder to confess, to which he acceded with the words, 'I am a guilty man'. He then produced a written confession, which he signed on the morning of his execution on 11 August 1828, but William always maintained that he did not stab Maria – perhaps her father's small mole spade, driven into the ground while searching for her, caused her wounds. The trial and execution of Corder drew immense national interest in the press; it became one of the most notorious murders in the early nineteenth century, with over a million broadsides sold, books, ceramic figurines and even a play produced about it that has been performed ever since.

## THE STANFIELD HALL MURDERS

The first crime to really capture the public's imagination during Queen Victoria's reign were the murders committed by James Blomfield Rush at Stanfield Hall near Wymondham in Norfolk on 28 November 1848. The crime was the culmination of a tangled web of avarice between Rush and Isaac Jermy.

Rush was a farmer with pretentions of being a country squire, but he had a long record of dubious deals and financial problems and was always trying to find legal loopholes and wrangles to get himself out of debt or bad financial commitments.

Rush met his match in Isaac Jermy, the Recorder of Norwich, who knew the law and finance and was not afraid to use this knowledge to his advantage. The mortgage from Isaac Jermy to Rush for his home, Potash Farm, was due for settlement on 30 November 1848. Rush had blown all his inheritance,

he had no more sources of money to draw on, and he was left with no way of paying the mortgage for the farm. On the night of 28 November 1848 he walked the short distance from Potash Farm to Stanfield Hall, where he disguised himself with a mask, wig and whiskers and hid in the shrubbery. When Jermy stepped out from the hall to take in the evening air, Rush shot him at almost point blank range. The masked assassin then strode into the hall and shot dead Jermy's son in the hallway, before wounding servant Eliza Chastney and Jermy's daughter as they fled upstairs.

Despite wearing a disguise, the bulk and gait of Rush were quite unmistakable and he was soon under arrest. Tried at the Norfolk Assizes in March 1849, Rush arrogantly turned down offers of legal counsel and opted to defend himself. He was often belligerent and attempted to intimidate the prosecution witnesses. When Rush presented his own defence he spoke for a marathon fourteen hours. His five witnesses were hardly worthwhile, even damning. Amongst them was Maria Blanchflower, a nurse at Stanfield Hall, who stated that she had seen the disguised murderer but did not recognise the figure as Rush, despite having passed within a few feet of him. Rush asked, 'Did you pass me quickly?' – an unfortunate slip of the tongue, especially in open court! After a deliberation of just ten minutes the jury returned a verdict of 'guilty' and Rush was sentenced to death.

The execution of Rush on 21 April 1849 drew a massive crowd and a special train was even laid on to bring up spectators from London. As executioner William Calcraft was adjusting the rope around Rush's neck, Rush could not to resist a last whinge and a voice snapped from under the hood, 'This does not go easy! Put the thing a little higher – take your time – don't be in a hurry!' These were to be Rush's last words. As the chaplain read the section requested by Rush – 'The Grace of our Lord Jesus Christ' – the signal was given and the bolt was drawn, releasing the gallows trapdoor and James Blomfield Rush was no more.

## THE BERMONDSEY HORROR

In August 1849, husband and wife Frederick and Maria Manning murdered Maria's former lover, Patrick O'Connor, while he visited their house at Miniver Place, Bermondsey for tea. Frederick Manning would later state in his confession that Mrs Manning had shot O'Connor in the head and that when he found him moaning in the kitchen, admitted, 'I never liked him very much and battered in his head with a ripping chisel'. The Mannings took what goods and cash they could from O'Connor and then buried his body under the kitchen floor, before fleeing. O'Connor's acquaintances soon missed him and enquiries led police to Miniver Place, where they noticed two newly cemented slabs on the kitchen floor. These were lifted and O'Connor's remains were discovered on 17 August. The Mannings were tracked down – Marie in Edinburgh, Frederick in Jersey. Tried at the Old Bailey on the 25th and 26th of October, they were both found guilty and were hanged by William Calcraft at Horsemonger Lane Gaol on 13 November 1849.

Maria Manning became known as 'the woman who murdered black satin' because she wore a black satin dress for her own execution; such material was shunned by English women for years thereafter.

MARIA MANNING.
*38 years Old.*

GEORGE FREDERICK MANNING.
*30 years Old.*

## THE FIRST RAILWAY MURDER

On 9 July 1864 Thomas Briggs, a city banker, was attacked, robbed and thrown from the carriage of a train onto the tracks between Bow and Hackney Wick stations on the North London Railway. Found alive, he was removed to a nearby pub but later died of his wounds. The crime received a great deal of press coverage, and a reward of £300 was offered for information

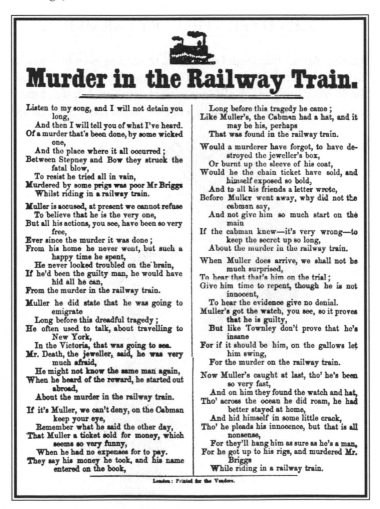

# Murder in the Railway Train.

Listen to my song, and I will not detain you long,
And then I will tell you of what I've heard.
Of a murder that's been done, by some wicked one,
And the place where it all occurred ;
Between Stepney and Bow they struck the fatal blow,
To resist he tried all in vain,
Murdered by some prigs was poor Mr Briggs
Whilst riding in a railway train.

Muller is accused, at present we cannot refuse
To believe that he is the very one,
But all his actions, you see, have been so very free,
Ever since the murder it was done ;
From his home he never went, but such a happy time he spent,
He never looked troubled on the brain,
If he'd been the guilty man, he would have hid all he can,
From the murder in the railway train.

Muller he did state that he was going to emigrate
Long before this dreadful tragedy ;
He often used to talk, about travelling to New York,
In the Victoria, that was going to sea.
Mr. Death, the jeweller, said, he was very much afraid,
He might not know the same man again,
When he heard of the reward, he started out abroad,
About the murder in the railway train.

If it's Muller, we can't deny, on the Cabman keep your eye,
Remember what he said the other day,
That Muller a ticket sold for money, which seems so very funny,
When he had no expenses for to pay.
They say his money he took, and his name entered on the book,

Long before this tragedy he came ;
Like Muller's, the Cabman had a hat, and it may be his, perhaps
That was found in the railway train.

Would a murderer have forgot, to have destroyed the jeweller's box,
Or burnt up the sleeve of his coat,
Would he the chain ticket have sold, and himself exposed so bold,
And to all his friends a letter wrote,
Before Muller went away, why did not the cabman say,
And not give him so much start on the main
If the cabman knew—it's very wrong—to keep the secret up so long,
About the murder in the railway train.

When Muller does arrive, we shall not be much surprised,
To hear that that's him on the trial ;
Give him time to repent, though he is not innocent,
To hear the evidence give no denial.
Muller's got the watch, you see, so it proves that he is guilty,
But like Townley don't prove that he's insane
For if it should be him, on the gallows let him swing,
For the murder on the railway train.

Now Muller's caught at last, tho' he's been so very fast,
And on him they found the watch and hat,
Tho' across the ocean he did roam, he had better stayed at home,
And hid himself in some little crack,
Tho' he pleads his innocence, but that is all nonsense,
For they'll hang him as sure as he's a man,
For he got up to his rigs, and murdered Mr. Briggs
While riding in a railway train.

London : Printed for the Vendors.

leading to the capture of the murderer. Suspicion fell upon Franz Muller who, when arrested, was found with Briggs' gold watch and hat. It transpired that Muller had picked up the wrong hat in error, leaving his own in his haste to flee the carriage after attacking Briggs. Muller was executed outside Newgate Prison on 14 November 1864 by William Calcroft. He was the first person to be executed for a murder committed on a railway.

## MRS DYER THE BABY FARMER

Amelia 'Annie' Elizabeth Dyer was a trained nurse who found a far more lucrative business in baby farming. Dyer moved around the country using many aliases to avoid detection but was finally traced after a baby wrapped in a brown paper parcel was pulled

out of the canal at Caversham Lock, Reading. The wrapping still carried Dyer's old address, and a witness had spotted her on the towpath with a parcel under her arm. The waters were searched and a further six bodies were found. Dyer had been carrying on her trade for about twenty years and it has been estimated the number of babies entrusted to her 'care' numbered dozens, perhaps over fifty. Many of their tiny bodies were never found, but, chillingly, when Mrs Dyer was asked about the identification of her victims, she replied, 'You'll know mine by the tape around their necks.' Mrs Amelia Dyer was executed by James Billington on 10 June 1896 at Newgate Prison.

## CHARLES 'CHARLIE' PEACE – THE BANNER CROSS MURDERER

Charles 'Charlie' Peace was a habitual criminal; a violent burglar, he was also a skilled musician but his violin seldom filled its case as he used it to carry his burglar's equipment. Between 1851 and 1872 he spent a total of sixteen years in prison. In 1876, Peace turned from burglar to murderer when he shot PC Nicholas Cock during a robbery at Whalley Range, Manchester. He also shot dead his ex-lover's husband, Mr Alfred Dyson, at Banner Cross as he attempted to intervene when Peace accosted his wife. Peace fled but was finally captured in the act of burgling a house in Blackheath in October 1878. Tried and sentenced for this crime under one of his aliases, John Thompson, Peace was recognised at Pentonville Prison by one of his old warders and was soon despatched by train to Leeds to face trial for the Banner Cross murder. During this journey, Peace made one last gambit to escape and flung himself out of the train window. The train was brought to a halt and Peace was discovered unconscious, having landed on his head.

Found guilty at Leeds Assizes, when all hopes of a reprieve were lost Peace confessed to the murder of PC Cock and was hanged by William Marwood at Armley Gaol on 25 February 1879. Truly a bogeyman character, Peace was the subject of many

broadsides and penny dreadfuls; even years after his execution, mothers would warn naughty children, 'Don't do that or Peace will get you!'

## MRS PEARCEY

Mrs Mary Eleanor Wheeler, aged twenty-four, is known to infamy by her alias of Mrs Pearcey (she assumed the name of Pearcey from a carpenter with whom she had lived with but never married). She resided at No. 2 Priory Street in Kentish Town and had among her love interests furniture remover Frank Hogg. Hogg also had a liaison with Phoebe Styles that left her pregnant. Feeling under pressure, Frank married Phoebe, but carried on seeing Pearcey and employed her in the marital home to nurse Mrs Hogg and the baby. On 24 October 1890, Pearcey invited Mrs Hogg and baby Phoebe around to her house for tea – they were never seen alive again. Later that same evening Mrs Hogg's body was discovered on a building site in Crossfield

**Mrs. Pearcey.**

Street. Her throat had been cut and the mutilations inflicted on her body were so horrific that word went out she had been a victim of Jack the Ripper. A mile away, in Hamilton Terrace, St John's Wood, an empty perambulator was discovered covered in blood. The body of baby Phoebe was found on waste ground near the Finchley Road a few days later.

Frank Hogg had not been too perturbed by the absence of his wife; he thought she had probably gone to visit her sick father. When he saw the newspaper report of the two, as yet unnamed, victims, his concerns were raised, so he sent his sister Clara round to Mrs Pearcey and the two ladies went to the mortuary to view the body of the woman. Clara recognised her sister-in-law instantly but Pearcey tried to pull her away, insisting it was not her. This strange behaviour caused the police to visit the Pearcey residence. Bloodstains were found on a kitchen knife and poker as well as on her kitchen floor. When asked to explain this, Pearcey vaguely answered that she had been, 'killing mice'. Mrs Pearcey was tried, found guilty and executed by James Berry on 23 December 1890.

## LIZZIE BORDEN AND THE FALL RIVER AXE MURDER

At about 10.45 a.m. on 4 August 1892, Andrew Borden, the President of the Union Savings Bank, returned to his family home on Second Street from his usual rounds at the bank and post office in the city of Fall River in Massachusetts, USA. Shortly after 11 a.m., Bridget Sullivan, the Bordens' maid, who had been in her room, heard Borden's daughter Lizzie calling to her that someone had killed her father. Rushing downstairs to the living room, Sullivan saw Mr Borden slumped on the couch, bespattered in blood and gore. The post-mortem examination would conclude that he had been struck ten or eleven times with a hatchet-like weapon. Neighbours came running, doctors were sent for and as they comforted the shocked Lizzie, Sullivan made a second horrific discovery in the upstairs guest bedroom. Lizzie's stepmother, Abby Durfee Gray Borden, was also found murdered, having suffered nineteen blows about the head delivered by a similar weapon to that used upon her husband. The local police investigating the crime searched the Borden house for the murder weapon and found the head of a hatchet in the basement, but there was no trace of blood upon it. A few days after the murder, Lizzie was seen tearing apart a blue dress and burning it in the kitchen stove. She claimed she had brushed it against some paint and it had been ruined. Andrew Borden was not a popular man, he had enemies, but the police focused on Lizzie as the prime suspect and she was arrested on 11 August.

At the trial, held at New Bedford in June 1893, members of the investigation team would later disagree about the discovery of the hatchet – one said the handle had been near the axe head when it was found, another argued it had been deliberately broken off because it had been covered in blood. In court, an expert would argue there had been no time for the murderer to have cleaned the hatchet. No other suspected murder weapon was ever found. The jury deliberated for an hour and a half before returning a verdict of 'not guilty'. Lizzie Borden died of pneumonia on 1 June 1927 in Fall River, aged sixty-six. She was buried with her father, mother and stepmother in the family plot at Oak Grove Cemetery. Lizzie was never able to escape the notoriety of the 'Fall River Axe Murders', as it became known. Whether she did or did not commit the crime is still hotly debated to this day, and the rhyme created all those years ago may still be heard:

> Lizzie Borden took an axe
> And gave her mother forty whacks.
> When she saw what she had done
> She gave her father forty-one.

## THE PENITENT MOTHER

Thirty-three-year-old Louisa Masset was the first person to be executed in Britain in the twentieth century, when she was hanged by James Billington at Newgate Prison on 9 January 1900. Accused of murdering her infant son, Louisa claimed she had handed over £12 and placed her son, Manfred, in the care of a Mrs Browning, who had just started a 'children's home'. Manfred was found later the same day in the ladies' waiting room of platform three on Dalston Junction Station, wrapped in a black shawl – he had been battered with a brick and suffocated. The shawl was traced to Masset and a witness stated they had seen her on London Bridge Station at a time consistent with her committing the crime. Masset said she was in Brighton at the time of the murder and the witness must have been mistaken. A waiter came forward stating he could identify Masset as having had a meal at his Brighton restaurant at the time in question. The jury, however, decided that she was guilty beyond reasonable doubt and she was sentenced to death; there was no reprieve. It is said that as the hour of execution approached, Louisa agreed her sentence was just.

## THE MOAT FARM MURDER

Samuel Herbert Dougal was a well-built man of military bearing. It seemed he was quite the ladies' man, judging by the number of offspring he had around the world (he served time in foreign stations with the Royal Engineers). Already married three times and imprisoned for forgery, he set about finding a new amour and soon settled into life with a lady named Camille Holland in Bayswater. Holland was ideal prey for Dougal; she had a small fortune of £6,000 at her disposal and a number of properties. After bigamously marrying, they purchased Coldhams Farm near Clavering, Essex in January 1899. A few months after moving in, Camille disappeared and Dougal claimed she had gone to London and, a short while later, he moved his legal wife into the property with him. Over the next couple of years Camille Holland's bank account remained active and her assets were sold off by Dougal. Talk in the area continued – what had happened to Camille Holland? Eventually the authorities investigated, and, ascertaining the irregularities

of Miss Holland's finances, they laid a trap for Dougal and initially arrested him on charges of forgery in March 1903.

Police investigating the Moat Farm site learned from witnesses that Dougal had been seen filling drainage ditches about the time of Camille's disappearance. Curiously, her faithful dog Jacko seemed particularly drawn to one of the filled drains, and, digging beneath where the dog sat, police discovered Holland's badly decomposed body. She had been shot in the head and the recovered bullet was matched to a pistol owned by Dougal. After a two-day trial he was found guilty of murder and was sent to the gallows at Springfield Gaol in Chelmsford on 14 July 1903. The hangman was William Billington.

## DR CRIPPEN

In 1910, a murder case was described in the press as 'The Crime of the Century'. Dr Hawley Harvey Crippen (aka Dr Peter Crippen), an American by birth, had transferred to England to manage the London office of the medicine company he worked for. His wife, Cora Crippen (stage name Belle Elmore), was a music-hall singer. Never an adept performer, she spent most of her time socialising and working as treasurer to the Music Hall Ladies' Guild. She had a wide array of friends who would frequently visit the Crippen residence at No. 39 Hilldrop Crescent, off Camden Road. Dr Crippen was never quite part of the party scene but he loved to be seen presenting his wife with expensive jewellery and furs in front of her social groups; behind his back the inoffensive doctor was frequently the butt of jokes.

**DR. CRIPPEN**

The social whirl and Cora's expensive tastes placed a strain on Crippen's finances. Her put-downs became more public and critical and, to supplement their income, Cora took in 'paying guests'; Dr Crippen was expected to bring in coal, help with cleaning, and polish their shoes. Mrs Crippen had indulged in affairs, and the pair had separate rooms; the doctor became 'a rather lonely and miserable man'. Crippen increasingly found solace in his secretary, Miss Ethel le Neve. Demure, quiet and kind, she was everything the doctor ever wanted in a woman. The doctor sent her a note stating that his wife had returned to America, and requested Ethel to hand an enclosed packet of papers to the Music Hall Ladies' Guild. He also wrote that he did not expect his wife to return. Although they did not become intimate immediately, nor did Ethel move into Hilldrop Crescent instantly, things moved at too quick a pace to be considered decent in Edwardian times. There was also the question of Mrs Crippen's whereabouts; her friends had noticed that Ethel was wearing expensive jewellery which they recognised as Ethel's.

Questions became accusations and Inspector Walter Dew of Scotland Yard went to investigate. The situation became too intense for Crippen and he fled for the Continent with Ethel, the couple being disguised as 'Mr Robinson and son'. Finding Crippen had absconded, Inspector Dew took the opportunity to search Crippen's house thoroughly and discovered human remains buried in the cellar, identified by scars (the head and limbs were never recovered) as belonging to Mrs Crippen. The remains were also found to contain poison. Warrants were issued for the arrest of Crippen and Ethel. They had no idea that the murder had been discovered when they boarded the SS *Montrose* at Antwerp for Canada. Captain Kendall of the *Montrose* had read of the case and recognised the suspicious looking 'father and son' and alerted the authorities by wireless telegraphy – the first instance of suspected criminals being caught by this means. Inspector Dew caught a faster ship and intercepted the couple. Crippen and Ethel were brought back to England and were tried separately. Crippen was found guilty and hanged by John Ellis at Pentonville Prison on 23 November 1910, whereas Ethel was acquitted. After brief success selling the book of 'her story', she slipped back into obscurity.

## BYWATERS AND THOMPSON

At about midnight on 3 October 1922, Percy Thompson, aged thirty-four, and his wife Edith, thirty-two, were walking back to their home at No. 41 Kensington Gardens in Ilford after an evening at the theatre. A man wearing an overcoat rushed up to the couple and pushed Edith away. An altercation between Percy and the man erupted into a fight, and ultimately the fatal stabbing of Percy Thompson. Edith recognised the mystery man by his overcoat as being Frederick Bywaters, aged twenty-one. The police investigations soon revealed Bywaters

## EDITH THOMPSON    FREDERICK BYWATERS

and Edith Thompson had been having an affair. Both were arrested on 4 October; Bywaters claiming he knew nothing about the murder and Edith bemoaning, 'Oh God, why did he do it?'

Soon, the love letters regularly sent by Edith to Bywaters when he was away at sea were discovered and their romantic content, accompanied by cuttings from current murder trials and mooted notions of killing Percy, was made much of at the ensuing trial. Bywaters' guilt was never really in doubt but the question of whether Edith really had plotted with the infatuated young man to murder her husband remains debatable. Thompson and Bywaters were both hanged

simultaneously at 9 a.m. on the morning of 9 January 1923
– Thompson at Holloway Prison and Bywaters at Pentonville.
Thompson's executioner, John Ellis, claimed that he was
haunted by the execution; he swore he would never hang
another woman and eventually committed suicide in 1932.

## THE PAPIN SISTERS

Christine and Léa Papin were reclusive sisters who grew up
and found employment as maids, usually together, in the good
homes of Le Mans, France. The pair had worked together in
the home of M. René Lancelin since about 1926.

On 2 February 1933, Lancelin had been expecting to meet
his wife, Marie, and daughter, Geneviève, at a friend's house
for dinner. When they did not arrive he was concerned and
returned home. He found the doors locked and bolted on the
inside; the only indication of life inside was the glow of a
candle in the maids' room. Lancelin summoned the police and
they managed to enter the house. On the first-floor landing
they found the bodies of his wife and daughter, their faces
beaten and cut beyond recognition and their eyes gouged
out. Upstairs they found the maids in bed together. They
admitted to killing the women in a fit of anger and indicated
the weapons they used as a pewter pot, a hammer and a
kitchen knife. In court they further admitted to clawing out
the women's eyes with their fingers. Evidence from medical
experts pointed out the younger sister, Léa, who was of low
intelligence, had been dominated by Christine to the degree
that her personality and will had become 'absorbed' in her
sister. Christine was sentenced to death, later commuted
to life imprisonment. While imprisoned, her mental state
rapidly declined and she died at an asylum in Rennes in 1937.
Léa was released in 1941 and found work in hotels under a
false name; she died in obscurity.

## THRILL KILL

Nathan Leopold Junior, aged nineteen, and Richard Loeb, aged eighteen, were young men from wealthy families, both studying law at the University of Chicago. They arrogantly believed they were 'Nietzschean supermen', capable of committing the perfect crime of a kidnap and murder. After several months of planning, the pair agreed their target would be fourteen-year-old Robert 'Bobby' Franks, the son of Chicago millionaire Jacob Franks. After abducting the boy, in May 1924, they attacked him with a chisel and rammed a sock into his mouth. The boy died soon after and his killers took his body to a remote area near Wolf Lake in Hammond, Indiana, where they doused it in acid to prevent easy identification. They then drove to a hotdog stand and had dinner. Having finished their meal, they dumped Frank's body in a culvert at the Pennsylvania railroad tracks. On their return to Chicago, the pair sent a ransom note to the Franks family. The body of the boy, however, was found before the family had a chance to pay the ransom.

A pair of spectacles with an unusual spring mechanism was found near the body; inquiries revealed that only three people had glasses with such a mechanism in Chicago – one of them was Nathan Leopold. He gave Loeb as his alibi but the story they had concocted fell apart under police questioning. Tried for the murder, the pair admitted that they had been motivated by the 'thrill of the kill' and the attempt to commit the 'perfect crime'. The boys' families were wealthy enough to employ Clarence Darrow, one of the foremost attorneys of his day, who advised them to plead guilty – rather than give a plea of insanity – and thus avoid a trial by jury. This plea, along with the mitigation given for their age, saved them from a death sentence and the pair received life sentences. Loeb died while in prison after he was attacked with a razor by another inmate in 1936. Leopold was released on parole in 1958 and moved to Puerto Rico, where he died of a heart attack in 1971.

# NEVILLE HEATH

Neville George Clevely Heath, aged twenty-nine, was a disgraced and discharged South African Air Force officer and sexual sadist. His first victim, thirty-two-year-old Margery Gardner, was found lying naked with her ankles bound and her wrists showing signs of being bound, on a bed at the Pembridge Court Hotel in Notting Hill Gate on 21 June 1946. Her body bore the welts of seventeen lashes, her breasts were savagely bitten and her sexual organs had been attacked. Pathologist Keith Simpson concluded her sufferings had been ended by suffocation, probably by a gag or pillow. Heath booked into the Tollard Royal Hotel, Bournemouth under the name of Group Captain Rupert Brooke on 23 June. He soon claimed his second victim, Doreen Marshall, aged twenty-one, whose body was found under a rhododendron bush in Branksome Dene Chine. Her body bore similar wounds to those inflicted upon Gardner but poor Miss Marshall had been even more horribly attacked.

Police had been on Heath's trail since the Margery Gardner killing and a wanted poster including a description and photograph of Heath had been widely circulated. When Heath walked into Bournemouth police station giving his name as Brooke and offering to help with enquiries into Doreen Marshall's disappearance, he was recognised from the wanted poster and taken into custody. When his hotel room was searched, a luggage ticket was found and his case was claimed by the police. Inside they found a riding switch with criss-cross thronging that left a distinctive mark upon skin and which matched the marks on both the bodies of Marshall and Gardener.

Heath's state of mind was debated at length during his trial; the jury were convinced he was culpable and after an hour of deliberation found Heath guilty of murder and he was sentenced to death. No appeal was lodged and Heath was executed by Albert Pierrepoint at Pentonville Prison on 16 October 1946.

# 5

# SERIAL
# KILLERS

The term 'serial killer' was coined by former FBI Special Agent Robert Ressler in the 1970s. Broadly speaking, a serial killer is defined as a killer (or killers working together) who kill two or more people over a period longer than a month. The features often common to such killings, as profiled by the FBI, include sexual motives, anger, thrill, financial gain and attention seeking. Although a number of the cases included here pre-date the common use of the term 'serial killer', the features of the following cases are all clear exemplars of serial killers.

## JACK THE RIPPER

During the autumn of 1888 a series of horrific murders committed in the East End of London were to disturb the nation, made all the more grimly fascinating because the murderer was never caught, though his sobriquet lives on in infamy – Jack the Ripper. The press in 1888, along with urban myth and subsequent authors, have ascribed numerous murders to this killer, but just five deaths are widely agreed upon by most crime historians and Ripperologists as being committed by Jack the Ripper.

The first murder was that of Mary Ann 'Polly' Nichols, aged forty-two, whose body was discovered in the early hours of 31 August 1888 on Buck's Row, Whitechapel. This horrific and apparently motiveless murder provoked concerns that an insane killer could well be walking abroad in the East End of London. Other, earlier knife attacks and murders were soon ascribed, mostly by the press, to the person they were now calling the 'Whitechapel Fiend', or 'Leather Apron' because at the time it was believed by many that the killer was a slaughterman. Inspector Frederick Abberline and his team were despatched from Scotland Yard to investigate the murder 'on the ground'.

In the early hours of 8 September 1888, the body of Annie Chapman, aged forty-seven, was discovered at the rear of No. 29 Hanbury Street in Spitalfields. This time the wounds and mutilation inflicted upon her were even more horrific. A letter purporting to come from the killer arrived at the Central News Agency, postmarked 27 September 1888. It taunted the police and threatened more killings; it was signed with the now infamous sobriquet 'Jack the Ripper'.

The Ripper struck again on the night of 30 September. The body of forty-five-year-old Elizabeth 'Long Liz' Stride was discovered by Louis Diemshitz at 1 a.m. in Dutfield's Yard, beside the International Working Men's Educational Society Club building on Berner Street. Only her throat had been cut; it was assumed the killer had been disturbed. Later that night, Jack claimed his second victim. Catherine Eddowes, aged forty-three, was discovered in Mitre Square, more vilely mutilated than any previous victim.

This night of horror was to become known as the 'double event' and was concluded with a discovery made by PC Alfred Long of H Division in the doorway of 108-19 Wentworth Model Dwellings, Goulston Street. It was a piece of material, torn from Eddowes' apron, smeared with blood and faeces, upon which the murderer had wiped his knife and hands. Above the apron fragment, written 'in a good schoolboy hand', was the statement 'The Juwes are the men that will not be blamed for nothing'. Sir Charles Warren, the Commissioner of the Metropolitan Police, attended the scene in person, no doubt fearing riots and reprisals against the Jewish population in the East End if such an inflammatory statement became popular knowledge. He overruled the other officers on the scene, had the message copied down and then gave the order to 'obliterate the writing at once' – a controversial decision that was to ultimately be a contributing factor to his resignation.

Once the 'Jack the Ripper' letter sent to the Central News Agency gained publicity, the floodgates opened for a torrent of letters claiming to know, have knowledge of or even purported to be from Jack the Ripper. Some were illustrated with lurid drawings and lots of red ink; among the most disturbing missives was one sent to George Lusk, Chairman of the Whitechapel Vigilance Committee. He received a small parcel in the form of a cardboard box. To Lusk's horror, upon opening the parcel he found the box contained a bloodstained letter and half a human kidney.

The final victim of Jack the Ripper was Mary Jane Kelly, aged twenty-five, who was found on the morning of 9 November 1888 in her rented room at Miller's Court off Dorset Street. The walls of the room inside were splashed up like an abattoir and on the blood-soaked mattress was a raw carcass, a mass of human evisceration that was once Mary Kelly. Those who saw this horror – seasoned police officers and police surgeons – never forgot what they saw at Miller's Court. The killer known as Jack the Ripper was never brought to justice and the quest to discover his identity continues to this day.

# THE LAMBETH POISONER

Dr Thomas Neill Cream was a serial killer. Born in Glasgow in 1850, Cream qualified in medicine in Canada and practiced in Britain, America and Canada; fleeing the countries each time he fell under suspicion for his illegal medical practices, such as abortions, or after suspicion fell upon him for his connection to the deaths of women by poisoning. He was prosecuted for administering poison to Daniel Stott, his mistress's husband, in 1881 and served ten years of a 'life' sentence in Joliet Penitentiary. A few days after Cream's arrival back in England he was up to his old tricks, convincing prostitutes to take a drink with 'white stuff' in it or tablets for supposed medicinal purposes. They died in agony a short time later.

Disappearing back to the States again, Cream returned to London in 1892 and convinced both Emma Shrivell and her companion, Alice Marsh, to sample his deadly wares. Less than an hour later both girls were suffering convulsions. They were removed to St Thomas's Hospital; one died on the way, the other a short while after arrival. Cream produced posters and letters making accusations to increase his self-importance by demonstrating his knowledge of these crimes. He was soon under arrest, however; a prostitute, to whom he had attempted to give tablets to but who had palmed them away because 'she didn't like the look of them', came forward. His trial was little more than a formality; Cream was found guilty and sentenced to death. On 15 November 1892, just after the hood and noose had been adjusted, executioner

Billington pushed the lever and Cream piped up with his last deluded statement: 'I'm Jack the ...', but the trapdoors fell open and he died with a lie on his lips.

## H.H. HOLMES

Herman Webster Mudgett, better known under his notorious *nom de plume* of H.H. Holmes (Dr Henry Howard Holmes), was a sadistic serial killer. He confessed to twenty-seven murders, of which only four were confirmed, but his actual death toll almost certainly runs into the tens, some placing it as high as 200.

Holmes was a graduate of the Michigan Medical School but he soon found he could earn money by killing his friends and wives and claiming the money he had insured them for. Holmes had run a small drugstore in the Englewood suburb of Chicago and speculated in real estate. In the early 1890s, Holmes acquired the lot opposite his drugstore, built a new hotel and relocated the drugstore there. Employing a variety of builders, only Holmes knew exactly what was in the three-storey building, dubbed the 'Castle' by the locals. This was a building riddled with fiendish contraptions and devious features; among them spy holes into rooms, gas pipes that could be controlled from Holmes's office (so he could fill just about any room with gas), and chutes that ran from the upper floors to the basements (so that bodies could be dropped down there). If alive, the victims could be tortured; if dead, there were kilns to cremate them, lime pits to destroy them and even acid baths to burn off the flesh and muscle. After committing these atrocities, Holmes would wire the bones back together and sell them as skeletons to medical schools and students.

The hotel was often packed with visitors for the World's Fair and Holmes could have his pick of victims. However, after trade at the World's Fair slumped, Holmes fled from his creditors to Fort Worth, Texas, where he had inherited a property from two sisters – one of whom he had promised to marry, both of whom he murdered! Insurance companies had become wise to scams and Holmes was finding it increasingly difficult to get them to pay out. In spite of this, he pressed on with a plan he had concocted with his associate, Benjamin Pitezel, whereby Holmes would find an appropriate cadaver to take Pitezel's place, his death would be faked, and Holmes would collect the insurance and share it with Pitezel. Holmes cut out the middle man and just killed Pitezel, along with his wife and two children. The police began to investigate and received a tip-off from a former cellmate of Holmes; they also investigated the places Holmes had been known to reside at – including the 'Castle', where they discovered many of his devious and deadly devices. Tracked by members of Pinkerton's Detective Agency to Boston, where he was arrested, Holmes was tried and found guilty in Philadelphia and was hanged at Moyamensing Prison on 7 May 1896. Before his death, Holmes wrote a rambling confession, in which he claimed to have murdered some people later found to be alive. The veracity of his claims about his life and murders remain difficult to disentangle, but it can be safely assumed that Holmes remains one of the most prolific serial killers of all time.

## HELL'S BELLE

Norwegian-born Bella 'Belle' Gunness migrated to America in 1876, where she soon married and settled in Austin, Illinois. Her career of crime began with the death of her first husband, Mads Sorenson, whose death was attributed to acute colitis, but who she had probably poisoned. Having got away with that and receiving a good payout from the insurance company, she began purchasing properties, they would suffer a mysterious fire, she would claim the insurance money, then move on and repeat the process. Her second husband, Peter Gunness, also had his life cut short, after a hatchet slipped from a shelf and struck him on the head – or at least that is what Belle told the jury, who believed her.

Gunness eventually established herself and her children in a farm about one and a half miles out of the town of La Porte, Indiana, and advertised herself in Chicago newspapers as an attractive widow of means seeking a gentleman of wealth and cultured tastes with the object of matrimony. She would correspond with the potential suitor and find out what relatives or friends they had, and those she believed would be missed least were invited to join her on the farm, bringing with them a monetary token of good faith. She would then kill the suitor, relieve him of his cash and valuables, and bury his body on the farm, usually under the hog-lot. Her grim business ended on 28 April 1908 when a fire swept through the farmhouse; the badly burned bodies of Gunness and her children were found within (Gunness was found decapitated).

Some of the realtives of those men who had visited Gunness became suspicious, and so an investigator and his team took spades to the farm and began to dig. The remains of about twelve bodies, mostly those of men, were uncovered but among them the corpses of one woman and two children were also found. Tragically, the methods of recovery were crude and only a handful of the victims were identified. Estimates place the total number of deaths at the hands of Gunness over the years at over forty people. Whether the headless body of the woman found in the fire was actually that of Belle Gunness has still not been proven beyond doubt and 'sightings' of her in other parts of America were being made as late as 1931.

## AMERICAN NIGHTMARE

While Belle Gunness may have the infamy, her death toll does not come close to that of Jane Toppan. Toppan had trained as a nurse at the Cambridge Hospital in Middlesex County, Massachusetts in the 1880s, where she began to use the patients under her care for her own experiments with morphine and atropine. Toppan would administer a drug mixture to the patient she chose as her victim, then lie in bed with them as she derived a sexual thrill when they were near death. After a brief sojourn at the prestigious Massachusetts General Hospital, she was dismissed and found work as a private family nurse. During this time she carried on her crimes, killing her landlords to avoid rent arrears, her patients, and she even got rid of her own foster sister with a dose of strychnine. Toppan obtained a place in the household of the Davis family in Cataumet, Massachusetts in 1901. Within weeks Toppan had killed the head of the household, the elderly Mr Alden Davis, and his two daughters. Surviving members of the family were dissatisfied with these sudden deaths and ordered a toxicology exam to be performed on Davis's younger daughter. Traces of poison were found and police arrested Toppan for murder. While in custody, Toppan confessed to a total of thirty-one murders. She is quoted as saying that her ambition was 'to have killed more people – helpless people – than any other man or woman who ever lived.' Found not guilty by reason of insanity, Toppan was committed to the Taunton Insane Hospital for life and she died there in 1938.

## THE ACID BATH MURDERER

John George Haigh was a man who wanted to live the high life of a gentleman, with hotel accommodation, flash cars and club ties, but he simply did not have the money and decided he could 'get rich quick' by committing a fraud, which landed him in prison. Next he tried murder for gain. He killed his first victims, Mr and Mrs McSwan (parents of one of Haigh's former employers), at No. 79 Gloucester Road in London. He placed their bodies in 40-gallon drums filled with sulphuric acid, which soon dissolved their corpses to sludge that he tipped down the drain.

Haigh stole the McSwan's pensions, cheque books and even sold their properties, raising himself thousands of pounds, and moved into the Onslow Court Hotel in Kensington. Haigh had a problem with gambling, which, combined with his expensive lifestyle, soon saw him running short of money, and so he found another couple to kill. On 12 February 1948, Haigh lured

Dr Archibald Henderson and his wife Rose to his small workshop at No. 2 Leopold Road in Crawley, West Sussex. When they arrived Haigh shot them both in the head, before he disposed of their bodies, once again in drums of acid. His final victim was Mrs Olive Durand-Deacon who, like Haigh, resided at the Onslow Court Hotel. Haigh took her to his workshop and sent her the same way as the others. Mrs Durand-Deacon, however, had a friend who became suspicious and reported her missing to the police. Mentioning her acquaintance with Haigh, the police looked into his background and his criminal record and had his workshop searched, which revealed Mrs Durand-Deacon's coat, along with papers referring to the Hendersons and McSwans. They also discovered a .38 Enfield revolver and eight rounds of ammunition. Pathologist Keith Simpson also conducted an investigation into some sludge found at the workshop and discovered three human gallstones and part of a denture, which was later identified by Mrs Durand-Deacon's dentist.

Haigh was arrested and charged with murder. He tried to convince the authorities he was mad, claiming he drank the blood of his victims, however, he was found guilty and sentenced to death. He was executed at Wandsworth Prison by Albert Pierrepoint on 10 August 1949. Haigh bequeathed his clothing to Madame Tussaud's Chamber of Horrors specifically for the wax figure they would make of him. He sent instructions that it must always be kept in perfect condition, the trousers creased, the hair parted and one inch of shirt cuffs showing.

## BLUEBEARD

Henri Désiré Landru was a convicted fraudster who took to representing himself, under a variety of aliases, as an eligible bachelor who would attract women with adverts placed in the lonely hearts columns of Parisian newspapers with promises to marry. He would ensure he gained control of his new beau's finances, then the unfortunate woman would disappear and Landru would move on to his next victim. Acquiring enough money to buy the Villa Ermitage at Gambais, a village south of Paris, Landru installed it with a large stove, thus creating his own cremation oven; the bodies of a number of successive victims were cut up and incinerated within it. Indeed, locals who passed the villa would comment on the black smoke that billowed from the chimney on occasion. Suspicion eventually fell upon Landru and he was arrested on 12 April 1919. A notebook found in one of his pockets revealed cryptic notes on all of his eleven victims. A search of Villa Ermitage also revealed some of their clothes and papers but the actual remains of his victims proved elusive, only bone fragments were found and Landru was totally uncooperative. His defence hinged on his belief that he could not be convicted unless a body was found and even when confronted by damning evidence he would reply that his knowledge of the matter was 'his secret' and that French law allowed him to remain silent. Despite this, Landru was found guilty and went to the guillotine on 25 February 1922 – he took his secrets with him. In 1967, a drawing given by Landru to his defence counsel during his trial was made public, it showed the kitchen and the stove and bore the following message on the reverse: '*Ce n'est pas le mur derrière lequel il se passe quelque chose, mais bien la cuisinière dans laquelle on a brûlé quelque chose*' (It is not the wall behind which a thing takes place, but indeed the stove in which a thing has been burned).

## THE MONSTER OF DÜSSELDORF

Peter Kürten was a thief, arsonist and a sadistic psychopath, who carried out a series of horrific sexual assaults, hammer attacks, rapes and murder of women and children around Düsseldorf, Germany between 1925 and 1930. Kürten's capture came after an encounter with a servant girl named Maria Budlick, who he took back to his home before offering to walk her to a hostel. As the pair walked through Grafenberger Wald he attempted to force himself on the girl and seized her throat. Curiously, he suddenly released his grip and asked Budlick if she remembered where he lived;

she said she did not and he left her alone. Budlick was able to lead police to the street where Kürten lived but she chose the wrong house. Kürten saw the police and knew they were on to him so he confessed to his wife and fled. She informed the police and Kürten was soon under arrest. Kürten confessed to seventy-nine offences and was charged with nine murders and seven attempted murders; he was found guilty and sentenced to death. While in the condemned cell Kürten revealed in interviews with Dr Karl Berg that the sight of blood was integral to his sexual stimulation and that it was his dying wish that he would hear the blood gush from his own neck when his head was severed from his body by the blade of the guillotine that he was executed with on 2 July 1931.

## THE BUTCHER OF HANOVER

Friedrich Heinrich Karl 'Fritz' Haarmann was a convicted thief, fraudster and child molester who, upon his release from prison in 1918, began a series of sexually motivated murders of teenage boys and men. When human remains were washed up on the Leine River in May and June 1924, police decided to drag the river and discovered more than 500 human bones, which were later confirmed as having come from at least twenty-two individuals. Haarmann was the prime suspect and was put under police surveillance. He was soon arrested after he was observed in the act of attempting to get a boy to return with him to his apartment. The room was searched and, to the horror of the investigators, a number of walls were found to be spattered with bloodstains. Haarmann tried to explain this away as the result of his illegal trade as a backstreet butcher. Clothing and possessions of a number of missing young men were found in the apartment and Haarmann soon confessed under questioning. He claimed to have been responsible for the murders of between fifty and seventy boys and men, but the police were only able to connect him to the disappearance of twenty-seven. The trial lasted barely two weeks and Haarmann was found guilty of twenty-four of the twenty-seven counts of murder brought against him. He was executed by guillotine on 15 April 1925. Haarmann's decapitated head was preserved in a jar by scientists in order to examine the structure of his brain, and is now kept at the Göttingen Medical School in Germany.

## THE BRIDES IN THE BATH MURDERS

George Joseph Smith had a long history of petty crime, going as far back as to his youth in the East End of London in the late nineteenth century. He married Caroline Thornhill in 1898 and over the next ten years he bigamously married two other women. Between 1908 and 1914 Smith entered into a further fourteen bigamous marriages under a variety of aliases. He would then draw off what valuables and money he could from each of these women and then disappear – he would also deprive three of them of their lives. Smith disposed of them in what he engineered to appear as drowning accidents in bath tubs.

His first victim, Beatrice 'Bessie' Munday, married Smith when he was under the alias of Henry Williams in 1910. He then disappeared, but Miss Munday saw him again by chance at Weston-super-Mare in 1912 and the besotted girl believed his

excuses; the couple were reconciled and made wills in each other's favour. Smith then bought a zinc bath and within days the poor girl was found drowned in it at their house in Herne Bay. The inquest had hardly concluded her death an accident when Smith was off again, but he made sure he returned the bath and got his money back before he left. His next victim was Nurse Alice Burnham, who apparently drowned in the bath at a house on Regents Road, Blackpool.

Death by misadventure was returned and Smith made £500 when her life insurance paid out.

In December 1914, Smith bigamously married Elizabeth Lofty under the alias of 'John Lloyd' at Bath and took up lodgings on Bismarck Road, Highgate in London. The day after they moved in, the landlady heard some struggling sounds from the bathroom and a short while later 'Mr Lloyd' was heard playing the organ. As water began to drip through the downstairs ceiling Lloyd appeared at the front door with a bag of tomatoes in his hand, which he claimed to have just been out to buy for Mrs Lloyd's supper. The pair went upstairs and discovered Mrs Lloyd dead in the bath. Death was recorded as misadventure but the case made the national papers and one of Alice Burnham's relatives saw it, was struck by the similarities between the two incidents and reported their concerns to the police. Smith was investigated and after initially being arrested for making a false entry on a marriage certificate, the investigation revealed his aliases and the charge was altered to one of murder. Found guilty, Smith was sentenced to death and was hanged by John Ellis at Maidstone Prison on 13 August 1915.

# THE RAINHILL MURDERER

Frederick Bailey Deeming was an unusual character. He was a muscular, hard-faced but handsome man and he was adventurous, having travelled throughout the continent, India, America, Australia and New Zealand – he had even worked on the gold fields of South Africa. Always flamboyantly dressed and supremely confident, he carried off impostures such as Lord Dunn and as an HM Inspector of Regiments. Those who knew the real Frederick Deeming called him 'Mad Fred'; he was a man who had carried out a host of minor crimes such as theft and embezzlements throughout his travels but had always managed to evade prosecution.

Deeming married an English girl and had four children by her, all of whom he left destitute in Australia. In 1890, he was back on his home territory of Merseyside, had a new residence at Rainhill and was courting pretty Emily Mather. All of this looked like it would be ruined when Mrs Deeming turned up with the four children. Explaining her away as his sister, Deeming sought a more permanent separation and smashed his wife and children's heads in with a pickaxe and buried them under the floor of the villa. Deeming and Emily Mather were soon married and on their way to Australia, allegedly on HM Inspector business. Within a few days of landing at Melbourne, Deeming murdered Emily and buried her under the hearthstone of their rented house in Windsor. When Deeming left, a prospective new tenant complained to the landlord about the disagreeable smell in the bedroom; the hearthstone was lifted and Emily's trussed-up body was discovered, her head smashed in and her throat cut. Deeming was traced and stood trial at Melbourne, where much was made of his mental state caused by advanced VD. It was said he went out hunting at night for the woman who gave it to him because 'he believed in the extermination of such women'. Found guilty, while in the condemned cell the story got out that Deeming had confessed to the 'Jack the Ripper' killings of Elizabeth Stride and Catherine Eddowes in London's East End in 1888.

Deeming was executed on 23 May 1892 in front of a crowd of 10,000; he contemptuously smoked a cigar as he mounted the scaffold. A cast of his head was taken after his execution and one of the castings was sent to Scotland Yard's Black Museum in London, where for many years the curator would indicate this as 'The death mask of Jack the Ripper'. Deeming was, in fact, in South Africa during the period of the Ripper crimes.

## 10 RILLINGTON PLACE

This is an address so infamous that a book and a film were named after it. Timothy Evans lived at 10 Rillington Place in the Ladbroke Grove area of Notting Hill, London, with his wife, Beryl, and their baby daughter, Geraldine. Money was tight and arguments between the pair were frequent. When Beryl found that she was pregnant again in 1949, she decided to have an abortion. What happened next is unclear but Evans travelled back to his native Wales and walked into Merthyr Tydfil police station, where he confessed to murdering his wife and putting her body down the drain at 10 Rillington Place. Police went to investigate but found no body in the drain; they did, however, find her body wrapped in a tablecloth in the wash house in the back garden, the body of Geraldine was also found with that of her mother. Curiously, Evans had failed to mention the murder of his child in his first confession. The case against Evans was brought to court and further evidence provided by their downstairs neighbour, First World War veteran and ex-War Reserve Constable Mr Reginald Christie, sealed the case against Evans and he went to the gallows on 9 March 1950.

Three years later, Christie vacated his flat and the new tenant, Mr Beresford Brown, removed the wallpaper sealing the pantry door in the kitchen and was horrified to discover a number of dead bodies within. The police were summoned and investigations revealed the three women to be Kathleen Maloney, Rita Nelson and Hectorina Maclennan. A further search of the building and grounds turned up three more bodies – Christie's wife, Ethel, who was buried under the floorboards of the front room, and Ruth Fuerst and Muriel Eady, a former co-worker with Christie, who were discovered buried in the small back garden. Christie claimed that he had lost his memory and went wandering around London, sleeping rough until he was recognised and arrested by PC Thomas Ledger on the Embankment near Putney Bridge.

It appears that Christie was only able to carry out the sexual act with semi-conscious and unconscious women. He would trick his victims into using an inhaler that he had connected to a gas pipe. Once stupefied, he would rape the women as they died, placing a ligature around their neck to strangle them if they appeared to regain their senses. Christie was only tried for the murder of his wife; he pleaded insanity but was found fully culpable and guilty, and was executed at Pentonville by Albert Pierrepoint on 15 July 1953. While in custody, Christie confessed to the murder of Beryl Evans but denied killing baby Geraldine. An enquiry was opened into Evans' trial and he was given a posthumous pardon in October 1966.

## THE BOSTON STRANGLER

In Boston, Massachusetts, the thirteen murders of women aged between nineteen and eighty-five, committed between 1962 and 1964, were attributed to the 'Boston Strangler'. Albert DeSalvo was tried for the murders, found guilty and sentenced to life imprisonment in 1967 – he was stabbed to death by as yet unidentified assailants at the maximum security Walpole State Prison in 1973. Subsequent research into the Boston Strangler murders suggests there may well have been more than one killer.

## FRED AND ROSE WEST

In one of the most horrific murder cases in modern Britain, builder Frederick West, later joined by his wife Rosemary, abducted, raped, tortured and killed at least eleven girls and young women between 1967 and 1987. Among the victims was Rose's stepdaughter, Charmaine, murdered to break links with Fred's first wife, and the death of one of the couple's own daughters, Heather, in 1987. The majority of the murders were committed by the couple between 1973 and 1979 at their home at 25 Cromwell Street in Gloucester. It was here, whilst Fred was being investigated for rape, police interviews with the West's children revealed that West would threaten his children by 'joking' about 'Heather being under the patio', which led police to obtain a search warrant to excavate the garden in February 1994. Shortly afterwards human remains were indeed found in the garden. Fred and Rose West were brought before the Gloucester magistrates court on 30 June 1994, where he was charged with eleven and she with ten counts of murder. Fred West hanged himself while on remand at Winson Green Prison, Birmingham on 1 January 1995. Rosemary West, however, was brought to trial and was found guilty of ten murders on 22 November 1995; she was sentenced to a whole life tariff by Home Secretary Jack Straw in 1997. Rose offered no confession but Fred West claimed to have killed more, indeed, the police are convinced the couple were responsible for more murders.

## THE SUFFOLK STRANGLER

On 22 February 2008, forklift truck driver Steven Wright was convicted of the murders of five young women in the Ipswich area between 30 October and 10 December 2006. Wright admitted to regularly using prostitutes; all of his victims came from the red light area of the town. Curiously, all of the victims were discovered naked, there was no sign of sexual assault and two of his victims were left deliberately posed in a cruciform position, however, at the time of writing, Wright has yet to reveal his motives for committing the murders. When passing sentence, the judge recommended that Wright should never be released. Wright is under investigation in connection with a number of other disappearances and unsolved murders outside the Ipswich area.

# THE FIFTEEN MAJOR SERIAL KILLERS

This list is of non-medical, political or military killers based on the highest verified number of victims of a killer working alone.

| | Country or Countries | Proven Victims | Active Years |
|---|---|---|---|
| Luis Alfredo 'The Beast' Garavito | Columbia | 138 | 1990s |
| Pedro Alonso 'Monster of the Andes' López | Columbia, Peru, Ecuador | 110 | 1969–80 |
| Daniel Barbosa | Columbia, Ecuador | 72 | 1974–86 |
| Pedro Rodrigues Filho | Brazil | 71 | 1967–03 |
| Gary 'The Green River Killer' Ridgway | USA | 71 | 1982–2000 |
| Yang 'Monster Killer' Xinhai | China | 67 | 2000–03 |
| Andrei 'The Rostov Ripper' Chikatilo | Soviet Union, Ukraine | 53 | 1978–90 |
| Anatoly 'Citizen O' Onoprienko | Soviet Union, Ukraine | 52 | 1989–96 |
| Alexander 'The Chessboard Killer' Pichushkin | Russia | 48 | 1992–06 |
| Ahmad Suradji | Indonesia | 42 | 1986–97 |
| Moses Sithole | South Africa | 38 | 1994–95 |
| Serhiy Tkach | Soviet Union, Ukraine | 36 | 1984–05 |
| Gennady Mikhasevich | Soviet Union, Belerus | 36 | 1971–85 |
| Ted Bundy | USA | 35 | 1974–78 |
| John Wayne 'Killer Clown' Gacy | USA | 33 | 1972–78 |

# 6

# MURDER MYSTERIES

## MURDER AT THE PRIORY

In April 1876, successful barrister Charles Bravo and his wife, Florence, were living in opulence at their home, The Priory, on Bedford Hill Road in Balham. They had only been married for five months when he was stricken with pain and vomiting, dying in agony three days later. The post-mortem examination revealed an irritant, most likely to be poison, present in his body. At the inquest, Jane Cannon Cox, Mrs Bravo's maid, claimed that Charles Bravo had said to her, 'Mrs Cox, I have taken poison … don't tell Florence.' Antimony had indeed been found in Bravo's vomit but insufficient evidence was found to suggest how it had come to be in his body and an open verdict was recorded.

Mrs Bravo was already a widow who had become very wealthy after the death of her first husband and there was much gossip about the affairs she had conducted in the past, notably that she had been the mistress of a well-known Malvern doctor, James Manby Gully. Rumour had it that she had murdered her first husband and had likely done the same to her second; all of this made great copy for both gutter press and broadsheets. These suspicions and concerns came to the attention of the authorities and the Lord Chief Justice quashed the findings of the first inquest jury. A second inquest was opened and this time the jury declared that Bravo had been murdered by poisoning, but the evidence pointing to any culprit was weak and no one was ever arrested or charged with the murder of Charles Bravo. Florence soon moved away and quickly faded from the media spotlight. She died the following year on 13 September 1878 – her cause of death was recorded as alcohol poisoning.

## THE PIMLICO MYSTERY

The death of Edwin Bartlett in January 1886 drew great national interest. A post-mortem examination revealed that Edwin had been killed by a large dose of chloroform found in his stomach; his wife, Adelaide, was arrested and tried for his murder. The case of the 'Pimlico Mystery' was to become infamous in the annals of criminal history, and the revelations of the illicit relationship between Bartlett's wife and her tutor, Revd George Dyson, scandalised Victorian society. Further gasps were made as the sexual proclivities of the Bartletts were disclosed in court, with explosive revelations such as no less than six contraceptive devices being found in Edwin Bartlett's trousers, as well as a sexual relations and family planning book being found at the Bartlett's Claverton Street apartment. Looking beyond the scandal, however, the case hinged on how the chloroform had been administered. If such a chemical had been given to Edwin Bartlett – by force or deception – it would have left his throat and digestive passages burnt and inflamed as it made its way to his stomach, but there was no evidence of this; the chemical was only found in his stomach. With no evidence to show how or by whom the chloroform was administered, Adelaide Bartlett was found not guilty. Famous surgeon Sir James Paget commented after the verdict: 'Mrs Bartlett was no doubt properly acquitted. But now it is to be hoped that, in the interests of science, she will tell us how she did it!'

## THE YARMOUTH BEACH MURDERS

Herbert John Bennett was hanged for the murder of his estranged wife, Mary, at Norwich Prison on 21 March 1901; he proclaimed his innocence throughout the trial, and went to the gallows in silence. Mrs Mary Jane Bennett had taken lodgings in Great Yarmouth under a false name in September 1900, and, asking her landlady to look after her daughter, Mrs Bennett said she was going to meet someone for a drink. The following morning she was discovered on the beach, strangled with a bootlace from one of her own boots. Bennett was the prime suspect but he swore he was in London. Among Bennett's effects was found a gold chain, said to match the one worn by Mrs Bennett when she was photographed early in her stay at Yarmouth. At the trial the eminent defence counsel, Edward Marshall Hall, argued that the chain in the photo was not the same as the one found in Bennett's possession (he never ceased to believe in his client's innocence). There was even a witness, Sholto Douglas, a stranger to Bennett, who swore he had met him at Eltham at the time of the murder, thus giving him an alibi. The jury still believed that Bennett was guilty and he was sent to the gallows. Many, however, believed in his innocence; it was even claimed that the flagpole snapped in half when the black flag was hoisted above the prison to

DISCOVERY OF BODY ON YARMOUTH BEACH.

indicate the execution had taken place – thought by many to be a sure sign of a miscarriage of justice.

Almost twelve years later, the body of Dora Grey, aged eighteen, was discovered on Yarmouth beach on the morning of 15 July 1912. She had been strangled with one of the bootlaces from her own boot. Her killer was never brought to justice.

## THE LUARD CASE

A murder was committed at Ightham Knoll, the home of distinguished soldier Major General Charles Luard, on the afternoon of 24 August 1908. After enjoying an afternoon stroll together, Luard's wife, Caroline, went to enjoy their garden view from the summerhouse while the Major General walked to the nearby golf course to pick up the clubs he had left there. Returning home at 4.30 p.m., the Major General was concerned when his wife failed to appear by 5 p.m. Leaving the house to look for her, he found his wife lying dead on the veranda of their summerhouse, shot twice through the head. Her rings had been wrenched from her fingers and her purse pocket was torn away. The police were summoned and, despite evidence given early in the investigation by the gardener, who said that he heard gunshots at 3.15 p.m., when the Major General was at the golf club, suspicion fell on the aged military man. Such were the rumours and attacks on the character of the Major General, that he could stand it no more and threw himself under a train. Caroline Luard's murderer was never brought to justice.

## THE WALLACE CASE

Liverpool-based fifty-two-year-old insurance agent, William Herbert Wallace, was called away from his chess club meeting to take a call from a prospective client, who gave his name as

R.M. Qualtrough and asked him to call at No. 25 Menlove Gardens East the following evening. Setting out from his home at No. 29 Wolverton Street on the evening of 20 January 1931, Wallace took the tram to the Menlove district. He found Menlove Avenue and Menlove Gardens North, South and West. Asking several passers-by for directions, he was disheartened to eventually learn he would not find Menlove Gardens East – because it did not exist! Trudging home, feeling duped by a cruel hoaxer, he reached his front door and found it bolted from the inside. Trying the back door he found that locked too. He called out to his wife, but after receiving no reply a concerned Mr Wallace asked his neighbours if they had heard anything. They suggested he try the doors again – the back door was now open. He entered the house and discovered his wife lying dead in the front room; her head had been horribly beaten with a blunt object (possibly a kitchen poker or an iron bar, which was used to clean under the gas fire; both were found missing from the house but were never recovered). In the absence of any other suspect, Wallace was arrested and charged with his wife's murder. The trial hinged on the telephone call he had received, whether he could have committed the murder considering the time factors involved, and that he had no clear motive to commit the crime. Despite a favourable summing-up by the judge, the jury were no doubt swayed by public opinion and press coverage of the case; he was found guilty, but the conviction was quashed on appeal. Wallace suffered such persecution after his release that he moved to Bromborough in Cheshire, where he died in February 1933.

## PHILIP YALE DREW

Tobacconist Alfred Oliver, from Reading, was subjected to such a violent attack during the course of a robbery on 22 June 1929 that he died from his injuries the following day. A witness saw a man near the shop on Cross Street at the time of the murder, another saw a man leaving the shop wiping blood from his face with a handkerchief – a man they thought looked like an actor named Philip Yale Drew, aged forty-nine, who was appearing in a show at the County Theatre in Reading at the time. Could Drew have been the killer, or was it just a man who looked like him? The coroner's inquest was more akin to a trial of Drew, even though he had not been charged with the crime. The jury returned a verdict of 'murder by person or persons unknown'. Drew's ordeal was over, but his 'trial by inquest' drew serious criticism and led to amendments being introduced to the Coroner's Act, but it was too late for Drew; the stigma blighted the rest of his career.

## A QUESTION OF IDENTITY

On 21 Decmeber 1908, twenty-one-year-old Helen Lambie, maid to spinster Marion Gilchrist, aged eighty-three, returned to her mistress's flat on West Princes Street, Glasgow after running a ten-minute errand. She discovered, to her horror, that Gilchrist had been battered to death. A neighbour had disturbed the murderer, whose motive was theft, as a diamond brooch was found to be missing. Oscar Slater, a local dealer in precious stones, was known to the police for his association with local thieves and receivers, and suspicion fell upon him when it was recalled that Slater had been trying to sell a pawn ticket for a brooch and that he had travelled to America very shortly after the murder. When he heard of the accusations, Slater voluntarily returned to Scotland to clear his name. He ended up being tried for the murder, despite having proven alibis at the time of the killing and proof that he had told people he was going to America quite some time before the murder. Slater was found guilty and sentenced to death. Lord Guthrie, the trial judge, was not comfortable with the conviction and organised a petition, which received 20,000 signatures, and Slater's sentence was commuted to life imprisonment.

The following year, lawyer and amateur criminologist, William Roughead, published the *Trial of Oscar Slater*, in which he clearly set out the flaws in the prosecution and attracted the attention of legal professionals. Roughead's book even drew the interest of Sherlock Holmes' creator Sir Arthur Conan Doyle, who published his plea for the unfortunate man to be cleared and pardoned in *The Case of Oscar Slater* in 1912. Authorities were reluctant to re-open the case and it was only after the publication of *The Truth about Oscar Slater* by William Park in 1927 that the Solicitor General for Scotland re-examined the case and Slater's conviction was finally quashed. Slater was released on 14 November 1927 and was paid £6,000 compensation; he died in obscurity in 1948.

## THE LOWER QUINTON WITCHCRAFT MURDER

Lower Quinton is a picturesque village near Stratford-on-Avon, Warwickshire. Its rural community once depended on agriculture for its income, and witchcraft and folklore for its medicines. On St Valentine's Day 1945 the body of seventy-four-year-old Charles Walton, who had gone out to do some hedging, was discovered at the foot of Meon Hill. He had been 'pinned' to the ground with his own pitchfork, his slashing hook stuck deep in his body. Upon closer examination the rough form of a cross had been cut across his throat. Local police found no clues to suspects; locals just seemed to clam up when asked for any details, so they sent for detective Robert Fabian of Scotland Yard. He uncovered a wealth of information which indicated that the locals believed Walton to be a witch and that his murder was motivated by ritualistic folklore – Fabian devoted a whole chapter to the case in his memoirs. Charles Walton's killer was never brought to justice, Fabian never got over not being able to solve the case and the local Superintendent, Spooner, visited the murder site on the anniversary of the murder, even well into his retirement, in the hope that one day another clue may turn up.

# ASLEEP?

Feeling the call of nature, lorry driver Sidney Ambrose pulled his truck into the lay-by near the village of Ridgewell on 3 January 1961. Walking a few yards off the road, the trucker stumbled across the half-naked body of a young woman lying under a blackberry bush. Within twelve hours the body was identified as that of twenty-one-year-old Jean Sylvia Constable of Halstead, who had left home saying she was going to a New Year's Eve party in London. She had been seen in a couple of Braintree pubs drinking with two men, David Salt, aged twenty, and USAAF Staff Sergeant Wills Eugene Boshears, aged twenty-nine, before all three went back to Boshears' flat at Great Dunmow. All worse for drink, Salt and Jean Constable soon went into the bedroom while Boshears remained in the lounge and drank more. Joined again by the couple, all three had more to drink before falling asleep in the lounge. Salt woke up about 12.45 a.m. and woke Boshears to ask where the nearest taxi rank was. When he left, Salt believed Boshears and Constable were both asleep. At his trial, Boshears claimed he only awoke when he 'felt something pulling at my mouth. I was not awake but this woke me up, and I found I had my hands around her throat. Jean was dead.' Panicking at what he had done, Boshears disposed of the body in the lay-by where Ambrose later found her. Despite doubts of the eminent pathologist Francis Camps on the possibility of the strangling being carried out while he was asleep, the jury, after a deliberation of almost two hours, found Boshears not guilty.

# THE A6 MURDER

Late in the evening of 22 August 1961, Michael Gregsten and Valerie Storie were in Gregsten's Morris Minor in a cornfield at Dorney Reach, Buckinghamshire when there was a knock on the car window. Gregsten wound down the window only to have a revolver pushed into his face. The man wielding the pistol claimed he was 'a desperate man' and that he had been on the run for four months. He forced Gregsten to drive into the field then spoke to the couple for a couple of hours. He then forced Gregsten to drive for about two hours, before eventually ordering them to stop in a lay-by at Deadman's Hill on the A6. Stating he wanted to sleep and would have to tie the pair up, Storie and Gregsten implored the man not to shoot them. He tied Storie's hands, then the gunman ordered Gregsten to the rear for a bag on the back seat; as Gregsten did so two shots were fired and Gregsten died instantly. The gunman then ordered Storie into the back of the car, where he raped her. He then forced her to drag Gregsten's body out of the car and demanded she show him how to drive. The gunman did not easily master the gears; he ordered Storie out of the car, told her to stand near Gregsten and fired the remaining rounds in the revolver at her in the darkness. She was found in the early hours of the next morning by farm labourer Sydney Burton. Still alive, she was removed to hospital, where she gave her statement to the police from her hospital bed.

The revolver used in the attack was discovered on the evening of 24 August, under the back seat of a London bus. The first suspect arrested by the police was drifter and gambler Peter Alphon, but Storie failed to pick him out from a police line-up. The second suspect was a petty criminal named James Hanratty. In the identity parade the line-up were asked to repeat a phrase used by the gunman and Storie successfully picked out Hanratty. At his trial Hanratty gave two alibis for the night of the murder, one that he was in Liverpool and another, which Hanratty told his defence team shortly before they opened, that he was in Rhyl. Despite anomalies in the case for the prosecution, Hanratty was found guilty and was hanged at HMP Bedford by Harry Allen on 4 April 1962. Hanratty protested his innocence to the end and many believed him; Peter Alphon even made a public confession that he committed the crime and a group of sympathisers styling themselves the 'A6 Defence Committee' set about clearing

Hanratty's name. The remaining exhibits from the murder were rediscovered in the 1990s after being missing for years. They were tested for DNA in 1999 and, after the exhumation of Hanratty in 2001, his DNA was found to match the samples from the murder scene.

## THE AXEMAN OF NEW ORLEANS

The 'Axeman' crimes were committed in New Orleans and its surrounding communities between May 1918 and October 1919, during which time the Axeman claimed at least eight victims (the press speculated he had been responsible for a number of earlier killings, some as far back as 1911). His crimes appeared motiveless; no money or valuables were stolen, and the only immediately apparent link between the victims was that they were all Italian-American. The attacks were all carried out in the homes of the victims. His MO was also very distinctive: the attacks came at night, the Axeman would take an axe from his victim's woodshed, before gaining access to their home by chiselling out a hole in the back door or entering through an open window. He would then creep inside and attack his victims (men, women and children) as they slept. An infamous letter purportedly sent by the Axeman, dated 13 March 1919 and published in the press, stated that he would kill again at fifteen minutes past midnight on the night of 19 March, but would spare the lives of the occupants of any place where a jazz band was playing. New Orleans was filled with jazz music like never before and no attack was carried out that night. The attacks ended as abruptly as they began – the mystery of who the killer was or why he committed the murders is still being debated.

## BLACK DAHLIA

Elizabeth Short, aged twenty-two, was an attractive aspiring actress known to some of her friends and acquaintances as

'Black Dahlia'. Her body was discovered in Los Angeles on a vacant lot covered with weeds on South Norton Avenue, halfway between 39th Street and Coliseum on 15 January 1947, by Betty Bersinger, a young mother pushing her baby in a stroller. It was a sight the poor woman would never forget. She thought the body was a shop mannequin but when she got closer she saw it was the naked body of a female who had been cut in two, her head had been beaten and her face lacerated across the mouth and cheeks, leaving it with a ghastly 'smile'. Police investigators and the medical examiner would conclude the body has been dumped there. Upon examination, her body showed restraint marks around the wrists, neck and ankles, her bisection was a clean 'professional' job; other lacerations were found upon her torso and her body had been drained of blood. The coroner's inquest concluded that Elizabeth Short died of shock and loss of blood, due to the blows she had suffered to her head. Despite masses of newspaper coverage and a huge police investigation, her murderer remains unknown.

## DID HE?

Dr John Bodkin Adams was an Irish-born doctor who opened a practice in Eastbourne, Sussex in 1922. Suspicions about his methods and the number of wealthy patients who had left considerable amounts of money and goods to the doctor stretched back to the 1930s, but it was only in 1956, when Gertrude Hullett died suddenly while under his care, that the police received an anonymous call, arousing suspicions surrounding her death. Police investigators brought in Home Office pathologist Francis Camps, who, focusing on the ten years between 1946 and 1956, examined the 310 death certificates issued by Adams and deemed 163 of them suspicious. Bodkin was arrested and was tried for the murder of Gertrude Hullett, with the murder Edith Alice Morrell to be prosecuted afterwards. At the trial in March 1957 the witness statements conflicted, even the prosecution's medical experts gave differing opinions. The jury returned a verdict of 'not guilty'. *Nolle prosequi* (in other words the prosecutor decided to discontinue criminal charges) was applied on the count of murdering Morrell. Adams had been acquitted of murder but was convicted on eight counts of forging prescriptions, four counts of making false statements on cremation forms, and three offences under the Dangerous Drugs Act 1951 at Lewes Crown Court in July 1957. Adams received a substantial fine and was struck off the medical register but a number of his most loyal patients continued to consult him. After two failed applications, Adams was reinstated as a general practitioner in 1961. His adoring patients continued to leave him legacies in their wills to the end. Adams died in 1983.

## 'BIBLE JOHN'

'Bible John' is the nickname given to the serial killer responsible for the deaths of three women; Patricia Docker, aged twenty-five, Jemima McDonald, aged thirty-two, and Helen Puttock, aged twenty-nine, between 1968 and 1969. He picked up his victims at the Barrowland Ballroom in Glasgow and earned his *nom de plume* after witnesses claimed they heard him either quote from or talk about the Bible. All three victims were killed in an alley or back court, where they were beaten around the head before he ripped open their coats, pulled off their clothes, sexually assaulted them and then strangled them with their tights. All of his victims were menstruating at the time; all three had sanitary napkins or tampons placed under their armpits or on top of their dead bodies. Despite an intensive police investigation, a description of the man and an identikit picture being widely circulated in the media, and the continued efforts of police investigators over the years using modern DNA profiling techniques on samples taken from the victim's clothing, 'Bible John' has still not been positively identified.

## ZODIAC

The 'Zodiac' killer murdered four men and three women, aged between sixteen and twenty-nine, in the San Francisco Bay area of Northern California, USA during the late 1960s and '70s. Two young couples were attacked in their cars when parked in lovers' lanes, another pair were out picnicking. The killer named himself 'Zodiac' in his communication with newspapers and taunted police authorities by sending letters and greetings cards, in which he also gave details that only the murderer could have known and even bloody pieces of his victim's clothes. In the final known letter, written in January 1974, Zodiac claimed to have killed at total of thirty-seven people. The letters often included strange and difficult to decipher codes, many of them concluded with an extended cross and circle symbol – some of these coded letters remain un-deciphered to this day. The Zodiac killer remains unidentified.

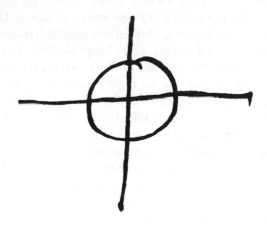

## JACK THE STRIPPER

'The Hammersmith Nudes Murders' of six (possibly eight) prostitutes by a killer dubbed 'Jack the Stripper', occurred between 1964 and 1965. The six definite victims of the killer all shared the common traits of the attacks; they were strangled, a number of their front teeth were removed, and their nude bodies found dumped at locations around London or in the River Thames. The only solid evidence found by the police on three of the bodies (this was in the days before DNA profiling) were flecks of industrial paint used in motor car factories. Police investigations focussed on factories and businesses where such paint may have been present and over 7,000 suspects were interviewed. Gradually the suspects were narrowed down to twenty, then ten and finally three, but evidence was never found to connect any of them to the murders and the real identity of Jack the Stripper remains unknown.

## THE 'SPY IN THE BAG' CASE

When GCHQ employee Gareth Williams had not been seen for a number of days, police officers were sent to check on him at a security service safe house flat in Pimlico, London on 23 August 2010. His remains were discovered in a padlocked sports bag in the en-suite bathroom of the main bedroom. Coroner Dr Fiona Wilcox stated that examination of the body revealed Williams had been dead for about a week when discovered, no injuries or signs of a struggle had been found, nor any evidence of alcohol or common recreational drugs. In a narrative verdict Williams' death was recorded as 'unnatural and likely to have been criminally meditated'. Despite a major investigation his killer, or killers, have not been brought to justice. The case remains the subject of much speculation and conspiracy theories.

# 7

# MURDER NOT PROVEN

A curious verdict beyond the usual 'not guilty' or 'guilty', and one that only exists in Scottish law, is that of 'not proven', whereby the judge or jury does not have enough evidence to be satisfied beyond all reasonable doubt to convict the accused, yet remain unconvinced of their complete innocence and will not return a 'not guilty' verdict. In British law such a situation can result in a hung jury, and in these circumstances a retrial may be ordered. If the situation occurs again after the second trial, a decision of *nolle prosequi* by the prosecutor may be called; in other words, the prosecutor decides not to pursue a further trial, the case is dropped against the accused and they regain their liberty. Two Scottish cases have become particularly synonymous with this curious point of law, those of Madeleine Smith (1857) and Alfred Monson (1893).

## MADELEINE SMITH

Madeleine Hamilton Smith was the first-born child of a well-to-do Glasgow family. She entered into a secret love affair with Pierre Emile L'Angelier, an apprentice nurseryman, and agreed to marry him. Unaware of this liaison, Smith's parents had found a suitor from their own class named William Harper Minnoch. Smith attempted to break off her engagement to L'Angelier but he tried to force their marriage by threatening to expose her using the love letters she had sent to him. A few days later, Smith went to a local druggist and purchased some arsenic and signed the poisons register – L'Angelier died of arsenic poisoning on 23 March 1857. Smith's love letters were discovered in the room where L'Angelier had been lodging and she was soon under arrest.

At her trial, the prosecution relied heavily on the love letters to build a case against Smith, but many of them were undated and reliance was placed upon the envelopes, which bore date stamps. It was soon revealed, however, that when the letters had been recovered they had been placed into whatever envelopes came to hand. Despite proof that Smith had purchased poison and that a motive for murder had been established, the case for the prosecution was so weakened by the collapse of the letters evidence, along with the lack of witnesses to prove that Smith and L'Angelier had met over the weeks before the murder, the jury returned a verdict of 'not proven'. Smith was released and died in 1928.

## ALFRED MONSON

Alfred John Monson was a private tutor for the Hamborough family when Cecil Hamborough took Monson and one of his pupils named Edward Scott (real name Edward Sweeney, a bookmaker's clerk from London and friend of Monson) on a day's hunting on the Ardlamont Estate in Argyll in August 1893. It was only when Monson and Scott had returned and were cleaning their guns that the estate butler enquired as to Mr Hamborough's whereabouts. Monson revealed that Hamborough had met with an accident – he had shot himself in the head whilst climbing a fence. It was initially believed to have been an accident until it was revealed Hamborough had taken out two life insurance policies just six days before he died – and Monson's wife was named as beneficiary! Monson was arrested and brought to trial, during which

Dr Joseph Bell (Arthur Conan Doyle's real-life inspiration for his character Sherlock Holmes) gave evidence and testified that in his opinion Monson had murdered Hamborough. However, Monson's advocate, John Comrie Thomson, argued eloquently against Monson being a killer, and a verdict of 'not proven' was returned and Monson was released.

Monson successfully sued Madame Tussauds in London for displaying a waxwork of him at the entrance to their Chamber of Horrors; however, he was only awarded the minimum amount in damages – one farthing. The law eventually caught up with him and Monson was jailed for an unrelated case of fraud, five years after his trial for murder. For years afterwards a notice was published in national newspapers on the anniversary of Hamborough's death stating: 'Sacred to the memory of Cecil Dudley Hamborough, shot in a wood near Ardlamont, August 10th, 1893. "Vengeance is mine, I will repay," saith the Lord.'

## CRIME OF PASSION?

Twenty-one-year-old Ellen Kittel became infatuated with one of the labourers on her father's farm at Great Bromley, Essex. There was a problem though, he was over twenty years older than Ellen and he was married.

During the harvest of 1871, Ellen was seen to take drinks out to Mrs Kittel and her children, who were working in the fields, after which they all vomited – it was blamed on the sloe berries they had eaten earlier. Taking to her bed, Ellen took food to Mrs Kittel for over a week. Mrs Kittel was discovered dead one morning in such a position to indicate that she had fallen out of bed. Ellen was in the house the morning that Mrs Kittel was found. At the inquest, Ellen's father was foreman of the jury and the doctor stated Mrs Kittel had died from the wound received from a fall out of bed. Ellen married Kittel just two months after his wife's death and then the village gossip started. The body of the first Mrs Kittel was exhumed and enough arsenic to poison her was found in her stomach. Ellen, who was heavily pregnant, stood trial for murder but it could not be proved she had administered the arsenic; the jury were sympathetic and did not leave their box before declaring her not guilty.

## MEET ME AT MIDNIGHT

Rose Harsant was a local girl employed as a servant at Providence House, Peasenhall, Suffolk, the home of Mr and Mrs William Crisp. Her father, William Harsant, came round at 8 a.m. on 2 June 1902 to bring her clean washing. Finding the back entrance open, he stepped inside to discover his daughter lying dead in a pool of blood. PC Nunn was immediately summoned, surveyed the scene and conducted a search of Rose's room for clues. He turned up a few letters, one arranging a secret assignation at midnight the previous evening. PC Nunn then called Inspector, who arrived at 2.30 p.m. and recorded the following:

> The throat was cut left to right severing the windpipe and left jugular vein, the flannelette night dress worn by deceased was partially burned as was also the chemise. A quantity of broken glass was found near the body (from a lamp she was carrying and must have dropped when attacked) as was 10oz Doctor Medicine Bottle ... A man named William Gardiner is suspected.

William Gardiner, aged thirty-five, was a foreman at the nearby works and prominent in the local Primitive Methodist Chapel. He was married but local boys had put about a malicious rumour that he and Rose, a member of the chapel choir, were behaving 'inappropriately' together. The gossipmongers got to work and in November William Gardiner was on trial at Ipswich for Rose Harsant's murder. Evidence presented did not convince all the jurors and they could not agree – eleven were for conviction, one

THE HOUSE IN WHICH THE BODY WAS FOUND.

ROSE HARSANT.

for acquittal. Tried again in the January the same thing happened – eleven for, one against. The case was declared *nolle prosequi*. Set free on 29 January 1903, Gardiner felt he could not return to Peasenhall, his name had simply not been cleared, so he shaved his beard off and disappeared in obscurity to London.

## THE HEIGHAM MURDER

On the night of 16 January 1905, a cry of 'Fire!' was raised at the home of Mr and Mrs Kowen in Heigham, a suburb of Norwich, Norfolk. Neighbours came running and the emergency services were sent for. Mrs Rosa Kowen and her children were soon rescued but her husband was not found so easily. Fighting through the flames in the small terraced house, firemen eventually found Mr Kowen between two fires – one in the grate, one on the floor. He had clearly been bludgeoned to death. When the fire was quenched, investigation of the house revealed traces of paraffin-soaked rags and a bloody hatchet was found in the coalhouse. Taken into custody, Mrs Kowen made just one very ambiguous statement: 'I did not plan to murder him, not yet to hurt him in any way.' Before the days of advanced forensics and in the face of the distinct absence of witnesses, there was no way to completely prove she had committed the crime. Was it sympathy or a lack of evidence which saw two trials and two juries fail to convict Rosa Kowen? A third trial loomed, and there was a public outcry that a woman should be put through such an ordeal again; every time she left the prison, crowds at the gates scattered rose petals in her path. An order to release Mrs Kowen was issued shortly before the third trial commenced. She left the prison in a closed carriage and caught a train to London. Just a few weeks after her release, she was admitted to a mental hospital, and she remained in care for the rest of her life.

## THE CAMDEN TOWN MURDER

On 11 September 1907, Bertram Shaw returned home to No. 29 St Paul's Road in Camden, London after a long nightshift as a cook on the Midland Railway dining cars. He soon discovered Phyllis Dimmock, the woman he had been living with for the last nine months, laying on the bed with her throat cut so deeply that it went down to the vertebrae. Shaw was to receive another shock, however; when investigation into the crime began it soon became clear that, despite her assurances to the contrary, Phyllis had used his absences for nightshift work to continue her old trade as a prostitute. Once her effects were searched, fragments of letters and a postcard signed 'Alice', with a cartoon of a rising sun, was discovered. The card was reproduced in the *News of the World* with the offer of a £100 reward for any reader that correctly recognised the writing. A reader named

Ruby Young recognised it as that of an occasional boyfriend named Robert Wood.

Wood was an engraver and freelance cartoonist; he claimed he used inexpensive prostitutes as his 'models'. It was thought he used the cover name 'Alice' to allay any suspicions Shaw may have when sending correspondence to Phyllis. Wood was arrested and positively identified as a man known to fraternise with Phyllis and her crowd in the Rising Sun pub, from which she operated, and another witness positively identified Wood as a man he had seen in the area of the murder on the day it occurred. Wood was ably defended by Edward Marshall Hall. Wood stuck to his story that he had only drawn the sun on the card to illustrate the mock invitation a girl was sending to her friend and with the hysteria whipped up for his innocence he was cleared of all charges. Hundreds cheered as he left the court but still the question remained – if Wood didn't kill Phyllis, who did?

## THE GORSE HALL MYSTERY

On 1 November 1909, a mysterious intruder broke into Gorse Hall, Stalybridge in Cheshire. The man, armed with a revolver, encountered the housemaid first; he swore that if she made a sound he would shoot her. She ran off screaming and the owner of the house, Mr George Harry Storrs, came to enquire what was going on. As soon as the intruder saw Storrs, he cried, 'I've got you at last!' and the pair grappled. Mrs Storrs also came running and managed to wrestle the revolver from the grip of the intruder, but he then drew a knife. Mr Storrs told his wife to go and ring the alarm bell but when she returned she found the intruder had fled and her husband dying, after receiving fifteen horrific knife wounds. Two suspects for this crime were brought to trial and both were acquitted – who killed Harry Storrs remains a mystery.

## THE MADAME 'X' MURDER

On 4 February 1929, Mrs Kate Jackson had just said goodbye to her neighbour after a trip to the cinema when she was heard to scream. Her husband discovered her laying a short distance from the back door of their home at Limeslade, near Swansea. She had been hit over the head and was removed to hospital, where she died from the injury a few days later, on 10 February. Police investigators found that Jackson had not been the novelist and journalist she claimed to be, instead she was Madame 'X', and the envelopes of cash she regularly received were from people she was blackmailing. Her husband was tried on the weakest of evidence and found not guilty; the real murderer was never identified.

## THE OTTERBURN MYSTERY

Twenty-seven-year-old Miss Evelyn Foster, daughter of an Otterburn garage owner, often drove taxis for her father. On the night of 6 January 1931, she was found badly burned beside the burnt-out shell of a car, which was still smouldering at a remote spot on the moors known as Wolf's Neck. Removed to hospital, she stated she had picked her assailant up as a fare, and managed to describe him as a small man in a bowler hat and a smart coat who spoke like a gentleman but with a Tyneside accent. According to Miss Foster, the man made a sexual attack upon her but she rebuffed him and he hit her so hard in the eye that she was rendered unconscious. The man then drove the car to the moors, got out, took something from his pocket, threw liquid over her and set the car on fire. With some difficulty, Miss Foster managed to crawl her way out of the car to the place where she was found later that night. Miss Foster died of her burns. The post-mortem did not reveal any evidence of a blow to her eye and suggestions were made that perhaps she torched the car herself as an insurance scam and the fire caught her. The inquest jury believed Miss Foster's story and returned a verdict of 'murder by some person or persons unknown'. The Otterburn mystery remains unsolved.

## THE BLACKHEATH MURDER

The body of domestic servant Louisa Maud Steel, aged nineteen, was discovered at about 7.40 on the morning of 24 January 1931, on an area of ground on Blackheath known as Horse Ring. Her clothes had been ripped off and she was left wearing only one stocking, both garters and fragments of torn undergarments. She was found to be gripping one of her court shoes in her right hand, as if she had been using it to defend herself. Within an hour the news was out and the press carried fears of another Jack the Ripper, but her mutilations were very different to those inflicted by the killer back in 1888 – no knife had been used, her killer had strangled her with the neckband of her frock and inflicted horrific injuries by stamping upon her head and kicking her body. No killer was ever brought to trial for this murder, but according to the senior investigating officers their number one suspect was a man (no name was given) from a good family who had recently been discharged from a mental home to their care. Immediately after the murder he was put in a state mental institution, 'no more to play the part of a scourge to society'.

# 8

# THE BLACK MUSEUM

The Crime Museum, otherwise known as 'The Black Museum', at Scotland Yard has a collection of thousands of items associated with murderers and murders both infamous and obscure; there are also other museums and private collections around the world containing items relating to murders. The following is a selection of some of the more infamous and curious curios of crime:

The bullet-riddled wall of the garage at 2122 North Clark Street, in the Lincoln Park neighbourhood of Chicago's North Side, where the 'St Valentine's Day massacre' took place on 14 February 1929. The wall was purchased by Canadian

*Scotland Yard's 'Black Museum' in the nineteenth century.*

businessman George Patey when the building was demolished in 1967. It is now on display in the Mob Museum in Las Vegas.

A bath tub used by George Joseph Smith, the 'Brides in the Bath Murderer', was put on display with his waxwork at Madame Tussauds in London.

A suit owned by John Haigh, the 'Acid Bath Murderer', was bequeathed by him to dress his waxwork at Madame Tussauds. He even left instructions that it must always be kept in perfect condition, the trousers creased, the hair parted and his shirt cuffs showing.

An account of the trial of William Corder, the 'Red Barn Murderer', is bound in the skin of Corder, which was removed and tanned by Suffolk Hospital surgeon George Creed following Corder's execution. (Moyse's Hall Museum, Bury St Edmunds)

The knife used by Richard Prince to stab William Terriss to death at his private entrance at the Adelphi Theatre, London in 1897. (Crime Museum, Scotland Yard)

The folding ladder, false hand, skeleton keys, violin and case which were used by Charles Peace, notorious burglar and double murderer, who was executed in 1897. (Crime Museum, Scotland Yard)

A Gold Leaf tobacco tin containing tufts of pubic hair from a number of women, which was found among the effects of 10 Rillington Place serial killer John Christie. (Crime Museum, Scotland Yard)

The tin opener used by Gordon Frederick Cummings, the 'Blackout Ripper', used to mutilate the body of prostitute Evelyn Oatley after he had strangled her in 1942. (Crime Museum, Scotland Yard)

The .38 calibre Smith & Wesson Victory model revolver used by Ruth Ellis to shoot David Blakely in 1955. (Crime Museum, Scotland Yard)

The bloodstained shoes worn by Francis Forsyth when he kicked Allan Jee to death during a mugging in 1960. (Crime Museum, Scotland Yard)

The tiny ricin pellet used to kill Georgi Markov by a mystery assasin in 1978. (Crime Museum, Scotland Yard)

The cooker and catering-size saucepans used by Dennis Nilsen to boil down the dismembered remains of some of his victims. (Crime Museum, Scotland Yard)

'Jacko' the dog (now stuffed) who led police investigators to the body of his mistress, Camille Holland, buried after her murder by Samuel Dougal at Moat Farm, Clavering, Essex. (Essex Police Museum)

The automatic pistol used by Madame Fahmy to shoot her Egyptian husband, Fahmy Bey, at the Savoy Hotel, London in 1923. (Galleries of Justice, Nottingham)

Bottles of Valentine's meat juice with water labelled by Florence Maybrick, convicted of the murder of her husband, James, at Battlecrease House, Liverpool in 1889. (Crime Museum, Scotland Yard)

The rope used by executioner James Berry to hang double murderer Mrs Eleanor Pearcey at Newgate Prison on 23 December 1890. (Crime Museum, Scotland Yard)

*James Berry.*

The 'Dear Boss' letter that was the first to use the *nom de plume* of Jack the Ripper sent to the Central News Agency in September 1888. (The National Archives, Kew)

The drug case owned by Dr Thomas Neill Cream, the 'Lambeth Poisoner'. (Crime Museum, Scotland Yard)

The bullseye lantern, home-made wick and piece of tartan cloth used in evidence against Albert Milsom and Henry Fowler in the case of the 'Muswell Hill Murder' in 1896. (Crime Museum, Scotland Yard)

The piece of tape used by baby farmer Mrs Amelia Dyer to strangle Amelia Fry, one of her young charges. (Crime Museum, Scotland Yard)

The photograph of Mrs Mary Bennett and the gold chain that were central to the case of the 'Yarmouth Beach Murder' of 1900. (Galleries of Justice, Nottingham)

The black cloth masks worn by Alfred and Albert Stratton when they committed the 'Deptford Cash Box Murders' in 1905. (Crime Museum, Scotland Yard)

Packets of arsenic and the diary owned by Major Herbert Rowse Armstrong, who was hanged for the murder of his wife by poisoning in 1921. (Crime Museum, Scotland Yard)

The rolling pin, dressing gown belt and towel used by Ronald True in the murder of Gertrude Yates in 1922. (Crime Museum, Scotland Yard)

The hacksaw used by Norman Thorne to dismember Elsie Cameron at his chicken farm in Crowborough, East Sussex in 1924. (Crime Museum, Scotland Yard)

The stocking masks owned by Frederick Guy Browne and William Kennedy, the men executed for the murder of PC Gutteridge in Essex in 1927. (Crime Museum, Scotland Yard)

The trunk used by John Robinson to hide the dismembered body parts of Minnie Bonati, which he then took to the left luggage office at Charing Cross Station in 1921. (Crime Museum, Scotland Yard)

The tin of Eureka weedkiller that poisoner Charlotte Bryant tried to burn and destroy, the evidence of her crime in 1935. (Crime Museum, Scotland Yard)

The polka dot scarf used by Leslie Stone to strangle Ruby Keen at Leighton Buzzard in 1927. (Crime Museum, Scotland Yard)

The whip used by sadist killer Neville Heath upon Margery Gardener in 1936. (Crime Museum, Scotland Yard)

The sawn-off Colt New Service .455 Eley revolver used by Christopher Craig to shoot PC Sidney Miles on the roof of the Barlow & Parker confectionery company at 27-29 Tamworth Road, Croydon in 1952. (Crime Museum, Scotland Yard)

# 9

# GLOSSARY

The following are terms used by pathologists and police murder investigation teams.

**Abrasions** – scratches, grazes, minor cuts or marks left by crushing or impact upon the superficial layers of the skin.

**Algor Mortis** – the cooling down of the body after death.

**Agonal Period** – the time between the lethal occurrence and death.

**Aplasia** – when an entire organ or a part of an organ is missing.

**Atrophy** – the partial or complete wasting away of a part of the body.

**Avulsions** – a grinding compression upon the body, such as a lorry wheel passing over the trunk or a limb.

**Blunt Force Trauma** – a severe traumatic episode caused to the head or body by a blow from a blunt instrument used suddenly and with great force.

**Cadaveric Spasm** – a rare condition whereby the muscles become immediately stiff after death.

**Contusion (otherwise known as a bruise)** – an effusion of blood into tissues due to the rupture of subcutaneous vessels, usually capillaries. Common causes of contusions are caused by a blunt force.

**Extra-Dural Haemorrhage** – an injury to the head, normally caused by a blunt force trauma that has fractured the skull with haemorrhaging occurring directly under the fracture.

**Forensic Dentistry** – the area of forensic medicine concerned with the examination of teeth, especially in the cases of victims who cannot be identified by conventional means such as a badly burned, disfigured or decomposed victim; similarly used to identify bite marks.

**Fractures** – broken bones.

**Fratricide** – the act of killing one's own brother.

**Incised Wound** – a clean cut or slash through the tissues of the body that is longer than it is deep. These wounds are commonly caused by objects with a sharp cutting edge, such as a knife or razor.

**Lacerations** – a torn, open wound to the body caused by an irregular-shaped object, such as barbed wire or a blunt force to the body that splits the skin.

**Ligature Marks** – marks left by an item that has been used for the purpose of strangulation.

**Livor Mortis (also known as Post-Mortem Hypostasis)** – a settling of the blood in the lower portion of the body, that causes a bluish or purplish red discoloration of the skin.

**Matricide** – the act of killing one's own mother.

**Oedema** – an excessive amount of fluid around cells, tissues or serous cavities of the body.

**Opisthotonus** – violent arching of the back associated with death by strychnine poisoning.

**Patricide** – the act of killing of one's own father.

**Primary Flaccidity** – the relaxing of muscles in the one or two hours immediately after death.

**Putrefaction** – the final stage following death, primarily produced by the action of bacterial enzymes.

**Regicide** – the act of killing a king.

**Rigor Mortis** – the stiffening of a body after death.

**Skeletonisation** – the process of decomposition whereby a body is reduced to a skeleton.

**Sororicide** – the act of killing one's own sister.

**Stab Wounds** – a stab or puncture that penetrates the skin and underlying tissues deeper than its length. Stab wounds can be

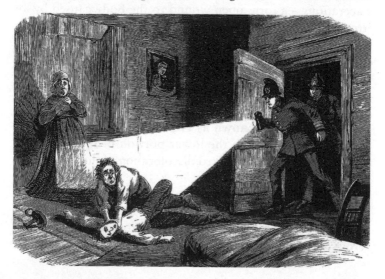

caused by a variety of sharp, pointed objects ranging from a needle to a spear or a screwdriver.

**Toxicology** – the testing of samples and investigation of toxic substances, environmental chemicals, drugs, blood-alcohol levels or poisons.

# 10

# MISCELLANY

## DECOMPOSITION

The more rapid the discovery of a murdered body the better the chances of obtaining clues about the killer from it. Decomposition can take place at different rates – a buried body can take years to fully decompose, while one left exposed to the elements and nature, such as flies, maggots, vermin and wild animals, can be reduced to a skeleton in a matter of days. A pathologist can use the decomposition of the internal organs of a body to help ascertain how long the person has been dead. As a general rule, the organs show putrefactive changes in the following order:

1. Larynx and trachea
2. Stomach, intestines and spleen
3. Liver and lungs
4. Brain
5. Heart
6. Kidneys and bladder
7. Skin, muscles and tendons
8. Bones

## THE TOP FIVE POISONS USED BY MURDERERS

1. Arsenic
2. Atropine (Belladonna)
3. Strychnine
4. Cyanide
5. Thallium

## YOUR LIFE IN THEIR HANDS

The following is a list of some qualified doctors who have been convicted of committing murder:

**Dr Buck Ruxton** – executed in 1936 for the murder of his wife and nursery maid.

**Dr Edward Pritchard** – executed in 1865 for the murder of his wife and mother-in-law by poisoning.

**Dr George Lamson** – executed in 1882 for poisoning his brother-in-law for financial gain.

**Dr Edmond de la Pommerais** – the French doctor poisoned his mother-in-law to claim an inheritance, and his former mistress to claim the money he had insured her for. He was executed by guillotine in June 1864.

**Dr Thomas Neill Cream, the 'Lambeth Poisoner'** – executed in 1892 for poisoning prostitute Matilda Clover. He is known to have killed another four victims by similar means.

**Dr William Palmer, the 'Rugeley Poisoner'** – hanged in 1856 for poisoning a friend to get money to settle his gambling debts.

**Dr Hawley Harvey Crippen** – executed in 1910 for the murder of his wife.

**Dr Norman Rutherford** – shot Miles Seton, a man who Rutherford believed was having an affair with his wife in 1919.

**Dr Marcel Petiot** – convicted of the murder of twenty-six people; he is suspected of killing as many as sixty. Petiot was executed by guillotine in 1946.

**Dr Harold Shipman (died 2004)** – convicted in 2000 of killing 15 of his patients by lethal injection, he is believed to be responsible for over 250 deaths.

## TEN UNSOLVED SERIAL MURDERS FROM AROUND THE WORLD

The Indian killer dubbed 'Beer Man', after the beer bottles he left around his victim's bodies, is believed to have murdered seven people in South Mumbai between October 2006 and January 2007.

The 'Lisbon Ripper' murdered three women in Lisbon, Portugal between 1992 and 1993.

The 'Original Night Stalker', also known as the 'East Area Rapist', is held responsible for the murder of ten people in Southern California between 1979 and 1986.

The Texarkana Moonlight Murders were five murders and three attacks committed by a mystery assailant dubbed the 'Phantom Killer', or 'Slayer', between 22 February and 3 May 1946, in and around Texarkana, Arkansas, USA.

The Highway of Tears, a section of the Yellowhead Highway between Prince Rupert and Prince George in British Columbia, Canada has been the scene of the deaths or disappearances of around forty young women in since 1969.

'The Claremont Murders' occurred in a wealthy western suburb of Perth, Western Australia, where the murders of two young women and the disappearance of a third occurred between 1996 and 1997.

The so-called 'Rainbow Maniac' is believed to be responsible for a series of thirteen murders of gay men by shooting, between July 2007 and August 2008 in Paturis Park, Carapicuiba, Brazil.

Hundreds of violent deaths suffered by women are ascribed to a single mystery murderer since 1993 in the northern Mexican city of Ciudad Juárez, in a case now known as 'The Dead Women of Juárez'.

'The Alphabet Murders', also known as the 'Double Initial Murders', occurred in the Rochester, New York area during the early 1970s. They were given the name after it was found that each of the three young murdered girls had Christian names and surnames that began with the same letters.

The 'Cincinnati Strangler' raped and strangled seven, mostly elderly, women in Cincinnati, Ohio, USA between 1965 and 1966.

# THE MURDEROUS MAJOR'S CONTRIBUTIONS TO THE OXFORD ENGLISH DICTIONARY

American Army Surgeon William Chester Minor (aka W.C. Minor) came to England and settled in Lambeth, London in 1871. Increasingly troubled with paranoia, Minor shot George Merrett, another man from his lodging house who Minor believed had broken into his room. Minor was found not guilty on grounds of insanity and was sent to Broadmoor Criminal Lunatic Asylum. While there he did not waste his time and after seeing an advert for assistance in research became a principal contributor of sixteenth- and seventeenth-century quotations for the new edition of the Oxford English Dictionary.

# SOME UNUSUAL MURDER WEAPONS

William Nelson Adams stabbed George Jones to death with a shoemaker's awl in London in 1919.

David Caplan beat his wife and children to death with a flat iron in Liverpool in 1919.

The exiled Russian Marxist revolutionary Leon Trotsky died at his home in Mexico, after receiving a blow to his head with an ice axe wielded by assassin Jaime Ramón Mercader del Río in 1940.

Harry Lewis used a tubular chair to inflict mortal wounds upon Harry Michaelson during a robbery at the latter's flat in George Street, Marylebone in 1948.

Daniel Raven used the base of a television set aerial to beat Leopold Goodman to death at Goodman's home in Ashcombe Gardens in Edgware, Middlesex in 1949.

Michael Dowdall battered Veronica Murray to death with a 6lb Weider dumbbell at her boarding house room on Chatteris Road, Kilburn in 1958.

A slice of Dundee cake laced with aconite was used by Dr George Lamson to poison to his young brother-in-law, Percy, in 1881.

According to a story recorded by Thomas de la Moore, King Edward II was killed at Berkley Castle in Gloucestershire in October 1327 when an assassin thrust a red-hot poker up his anus.

In 1957, Mary Elizabeth Wilson, the 'Widow of Windy Nook' in Felling-on-Tyne, administered poison containing phosphorous to both her husband and her lover, either in the form of cough medicine or tea. When the bodies were exhumed they were found to glow!

A glass of champagne – laced with cyanide – was used by Harlow Fraden to kill both his parents at their New York apartment in 1953.

Stanley Wren smashed his boyfriend's skull with a gas ring he had dismantled from a cooker at College Road, Bromley, Kent in 1966.

John Donald Merrett battered his mother-in-law, Lady Mary Menzies, with a mock-pewter coffee pot before strangling her at her home in Ealing, London in 1954.

Edgar Edwards beat John Darby, Darby's wife and their daughter to death with an 8lb sash weight during a robbery at the Darby's shop in Camberwell, London in 1902.

Michael Queripel used a heavy iron tee marker to fell Elizabeth Currell, and then strangled her with a stocking on Potters Bar golf course in Hertfordshire, in 1955.

## THE FIRST CONVICTION
## BASED ON FINGERPRINT EVIDENCE

The first conviction based on fingerprint evidence in a British court of law was when Alfred and Albert Stratton were

convicted of the murder of Mr Thomas
Farrow in 1905. Alfred Stratton's bloody
thumbprint was recovered from the cashbox
he had robbed with his brother, after beating
elderly Deptford shop owner Thomas Farrow
to death.

## THE M'NAGHTEN RULES

On 25 January 1843, Edward Drummond was shot by Daniel
M'Naghten, who mistook him for Prime Minister Robert Peel.
Drummond died of the wound but M'Naghten was found not
culpable on the grounds of insanity. In the aftermath of the
trial, the House of Lords developed a set of rules that would
become the basis for the insanity defence in all common law
countries, known as the M'Naghten Rules.

## LONGEST SERVING PRISONER FOR MURDER

When John Thomas Straffen died at Frankland Prison in County
Durham in November 2007, he was the longest-serving prisoner
in British legal history. Straffen had killed two young girls in the
summer of 1951. Found to be unfit to plead, he was committed
to Broadmoor Hospital. Straffen escaped in 1952 and killed
again. Tried for this crime he was found guilty of murder and
sentenced to death. Reprieved because of his mental state, his
sentence was commuted to life imprisonment and he remained
in prison until his death some fifty-five years later.

## TRIAL BY BATTLE

One of the strangest murder cases occurred after a jury acquitted
Abraham Thornton, aged twenty-four, of the rape and murder of
Mary Ashford, aged twenty, whose body was found in a pit near
Erdington in Sutton Coldfield, Warwickshire on 26 May 1817.

Public opinion had been against Thornton; it was claimed in court that Thornton had callously stated that he had been intimate with Mary's sister three times, and 'would also be with Mary Ashford, or he would die for it'. Thornton later denied this statement. Mary's family were also convinced of his guilt so her brother, William Ashford, launched an appeal and Thornton was arrested once again. Thornton then claimed the right to use the unrepealed medieval law of trial by battle to settle the matter, a claim upheld by the Court of King's Bench! Mr Ashford declined to enter into combat with Thornton and he was released from custody and soon fled abroad. The public were outraged and the old law was soon repealed from the statutes.

## COINCIDENCE

In May 1983, workmen digging in the Cheshire peat bog of Lindow Moss discovered a human skull. When he heard the news, Peter Reyn-Bardt panicked that they had discovered the remains of the wife he had killed and buried in that area back in 1960 and confessed to her murder. One month before the trial, experts from Oxford radiocarbon dated the skull and were confident that the skull belonged to a woman who died about 130–290 AD (un-calibrated). Despite this development, Reyn-Bardt was found guilty of murder and sentenced to life imprisonment on the strength of his confession.

## CRIME CAPITALS

Based on the statistics supplied to the United Nations Office on Drugs and Crime (UNODC), the following are the recent homicide rates per 100,000 population in twenty countries:

| Country | Murders in One Year | Rate |
|---|---|---|
| Afghanistan | 712 | 2.4 |
| Angola | 3,426 | 19 |
| Argentina | 2,215 | 5.5 |

| | | |
|---|---|---|
| Belgium | 185 | 1.7 |
| Brazil | 43,909 | 22.7 |
| China | 14,811 | 1.1 |
| Colombia | 15,459 | 33.4 |
| Ethiopia | 20,239 | 25.5 |
| France | 839 | 1.4 |
| Germany | 690 | 0.8 |
| India | 40,752 | 3.4 |
| Italy | 590 | 1 |
| Japan | 646 | 0.5 |
| Jamaica | 1,428 | 52.1 |
| Mexico | 20,585 | 18.1 |
| Russian Federation | 15,954 | 11.2 |
| South Africa | 16,834 | 33.8 |
| Uganda | 11,373 | 36.3 |
| USA | 15,241 | 5 |
| United Kingdom | 724 | 1.2 |

The five London boroughs where the highest numbers of murders were committed over the years 2000/01 – 2008/09 were:

Lambeth (123)
Southwark (96)
Newham (95)
Hackney (94)
Brent (77)

According to official statistics in 2010, Scotland is the murder capital of Great Britain. It was also noted that the majority of the killings north of the border were carried out with knives.

Glasgow was dubbed the 'murder capital of Europe' in 2003. The Scottish Executive revealed that in 2002 there were 125 incidents which resulted in killings; forty of them in Glasgow alone, with 127 people dying as a result. The majority of victims were stabbed to death by friends or relatives who were in a drunken rage.

# 11

# LAST WORDS

The following are epitaphs carved upon the headstones and memorials of murder victims (and murderers).

> Unto the mournful fate of young John Moore,
> Who fell a victim to some villain's power;
> In Richmond Lane, near to Aske Hall, tis said,
> There was his life most cruelly betray'd.
> Shot with a gun by some abandon'd rake,
> Then knock'd out with a hedging stake,
> His soul, I trust, is blest above,
> There to enjoy eternal rest and love;
> Then let us pray his murderer to discover,
> That he to justice may be brought over.

John Moore of Gilling, near Richmond, North Yorkshire was shot from his horse on the road between Richmond and Aske as he was returning from market in 1758. His murderer was never brought to justice.

> HERE lieth the Body of
> Sarah Smith Daughter of
> Samuel and Martha Smith
> of Bradwall Park who
> departed this life Nover 29th 1763
> and in the 21st Year of her Age

It was C......s B.....w
That brought me to my end
Dear parents, mourn not for me
For God will stand my friend.
With half a pint of Poyson
He came to visit me
Write this on my grave
That all who read may see.

From the gravestone of Sarah Smith in Wolstanton, Staffordshire, who died in 1763. The precise identity of C...s B...w remains a mystery.

To the memory of Henry Scarles who was valued when alive, and respected now dead, was cruelly murdered at Whitacre, Burgh on 10th of February 1787 in the 23rd year of his age.

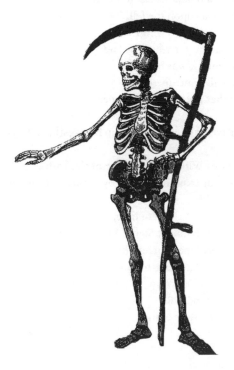

Scarles was a servant of Mattias Kerrison, a merchant at the staithe at Bungay, Suffolk. On the night of 10 February 1787, William Hawke of Beccles and Thomas Mayhew of Bungay, along with accomplice Simon Stannard, were robbing one of Kerrison's corn lighters when they were disturbed by Scarles. The robbers beat Scarles, pushed him into the water and struck him on the head with a quant while he was struggling. Laying low in the locality the felons were apprehended at Botesdale by 'persons employed by the Bungay Association'. Taken to Norwich Castle, Stannard turned King's Evidence and saw Hawke and Mayhew found guilty and hanged on Norwich Castle Hill the following March.

> In memory of Robert Baxter, of Far-house,
> who died Oct 4 1796, aged 56.
> All you who please these lines to read,
> It will cause a tender hearts to bleed;
> I murdered was upon the fell,
> And by the man I knew full well;
> By bread and butter which he laid,
> I being harmless, was betrayed.
> I hope he will remembered be
> That laid that poison there for me.

From the grave of Robert Baxter in Knaresdale, Northumberland.

> In memory of William Webb, late of the 15th D'ns,
> who was shot from his Horse by a party of Smugglers on the
> 26 of Sepr. 1784
> I am not dead but sleepeth here,
> And when the Trumpet Sound I will appear
> Four balls thro' me Pearced there way:
> Hard it was. I'd no time to pray
> This stone that here you
> Do see My Comerades
> Erected for the sake of me.

A short distance from Dragoon Webb is the grave of William Green, who died the following day of the wounds he received in the same ambush:

> Here lie the mangled remains of poor William Green, an Honest Officer of the Government, who in the faithful discharge of his duty was inhumanely murdered by a gang of Smugglers in this Parish, September 27th, 1784.

William Kemble, the leader of the murderous band of smugglers who killed both Webb and Green, was captured and brought before the assizes, but despite strong evidence against him the jurors failed to convict him.  Both graves can be found in Old Hunstanton, Norfolk

> In memory of
> A generous but unfortunate Sailor
> Who was barbarously murder'd on Hindhead
> On September 24th 1786
> By three Villains
> After he had liberally treated them
> And promised them his farther assistance
> On the road to Portsmouth.
>
> When pitying Eyes to see my grave shall come
> And with a generous tear bedew my tomb
> Here shall they read my melancholy Fate.
> In perfect Health and in flower of Age
> Fell victim to three Ruffians Rage,
> On bended knees I mercy strove to obtain.
> Their thrift and Blood made all Entreaties vain.
> No dear relation or still dearer Friend
> Weeps my hard lot or miserable End
> Yet o'er my sad Remains (my Name unknown)
> A generous Public have inscribed this Stone.

The above is from a gravestone in Thursley, Surrey.

Although the name of the sailor in the following epitaph was never discovered, his murderers were brought to justice.

> *ERECTED*
> In detestation of a barbarous Murder
> Committed here on an unknown Sailor
> On Sep, 24th 1786
> By Edwd. Lonegon, Mich. Casey & Jas. Marshall
> Who were all taken he same day
> And hung in Chains near this place
> Whoso sheddeth Man's Blood by Man shall his
> Blood be shed. Gen Chap 9 Ver 6

The reverse of this stone contains a stern warning:

> THIS STONE
> was Erected
> by order and at
> the cost of
> James Stilwell Esqr.
> Of
> Cosford
> 1786
> Cursed be the Man who injureth
> or removeth this Stone.

The 'Sailor's Stone' is near Hindhead on the old coaching road from London to Portsmouth.

> Joseph Glendowing
> Murdered near this town June 15, 1808
> His murderers were never discovered.
> You villains! If this stone you see
> Remember that you murdered me
> You bruised my head and pierced my heart
> Also my bowels did suffer part.

The above epitaph is from a gravestone in Workington, Cumbria.

Here lieth Martin Elphinstone
Who with his sword did cut in sunder
The daughter of Sir Harry Crispe
who did his daughter marry.
She was fat and fulsome,
But men will sometimes
Eat bacon with their beans
And love the fat as well as lean.

The above epitaph is from a gravestone in Alnwick, Northumberland.

To the Memory of Mary Morgan,
who young and beautiful, endowed
with a good understanding and
disposition, but unenlightened by the
sacred truths of Christianity became
the victim of sin and shame and
was condemned to an ignominious
death on the 11th April 1805,
for the Murder of her bastard Child.

Rous'd to a first sense of guilt and
remorse by the eloquent and humane
exertions of her benevolent Judge,
Mr Justice Hardinge, she underwent
the Sentence of the Law on the
following Thursday with unfeigned
repentance and a furvent hope of
forgiveness through the merits of a
redeeming intercessor.

This stone is erected not merely to
perpetuate the remembrance of a
departed penitent, but to remind the
living of the frailty of human nature
when unsupported by religion.

A second, less sanctimonious stone was erected nearby:

In Memory of MARY MORGAN who Suffer'd April 13th, 1805. Aged 17 years. He that is without sin among you Let him first cast a stone at her. The 8th Chapr. of John, part of ye 7th vr.

From a grave at Presteigne, Powys, Wales.

Here I lies
Killed by the XIS

Grave of an unknown smuggler, Woodbridge, Suffolk.

As a warning to female virtue and a humble monument to female chastity this stone marks the grave of Mary Ashford who on the twentieth year of her age having incautiously repaired to a scene of amusement without proper protection was brutally murdered on 27th May 1817.

Lovely and chaste as is the primrose pale,
Rifled of virgin sweetness by the gale;
Mary, the wretch who thee remorseless slew,
Avenging wrath, which sleeps not, will pursue;
For though the deed of blood be veiled in night,
Will not the judge of all earth do right,
Fair, blighted flower, the muse that weeps thy doom
Rais'd o'er thy murdered form this warning tomb.

From a grave at Sutton Coldfield, Warwickshire. Abraham Thornton, the prime suspect for the rape and murder of Mary Ashford, was tried at Warwickshire Assizes but was acquitted.

Alexander M'Donald
Late soldier in the first battalion 79th regt. Who in the prime of life was inhumanely murdered near Little Clacton on the morning of the 26th July 1806.

From a grave at Weeley, Essex.

Sacred to the Memory of Rev JOSHUA WATERHOUSE
B.D. Nearly 40 years Fellow of Catherine Hall, Cambridge,
Chaplain to His Majesty, Rector of this Parish & of Coton, near
Cambridge, who was inhumanly murdered in this parsonage
about ten o'clock on the morning of July 3rd 1827, aged 81.

Beneath this Tomb his Mangled body's laid,
Cut, stabb'd & Murdered by Joshua Slade;
His ghastly wounds a horrid sight to see
And hurled at once into Eternity.
What faults you've seen in him take care to shun
And look at home, enough there's to be done;
Death does not always warning give
Therefore be carefull how you live.

From a grave at Great Stukeley, Huntingdonshire.

Through poison strong he was cut off
And brought to death at last;
It was by his apprentice girl,
On whom there's sentence past,
Oh! May all people warning take,
For she was burned at the stake.

Headstone of Richard Jarvis, East Portlemouth, Devon, who
was murdered by his young apprentice, Rebecca Downing
(aged about sixteen) in 1782. She was burned at the stake for
this crime under the law of Petty Treason at Exeter.

Sacred
To The Memory of
THOMAS DEPLEDGE
Who was murdered at Darfield
On the 11 October 1841
At midnight dear by this wayside
A murdered man poor DEPLEDGE died,
The guiltless victim of a blow
Aimed to have brought another low,

From men whom he had never harmed
By hate and drunken passions warmed.
Now learn to shun the youth's fresh spring
The courses which to ruin bring.

From a grave in All Saints' Church in Frickley, Doncaster, South Yorkshire.

# 12

# A DATE WITH MURDER

## JANUARY

**1 January 1886** 'The Pimlico Mystery' – Edwin Bartlett is found dead at his home on Claverton Street, killed by a large dose of chloroform found in his stomach. His wife Adelaide was tried and found not guilty. Sir James Paget commented after the verdict, 'Mrs Bartlett was no doubt properly acquitted. But now it is to be hoped that, in the interests of science, she will tell us how she did it!'

**2 January 1956** The body of Anne Kneilands was found on an East Kilbride golf course, she had been raped and bludgeoned to death with a length of iron. Peter Manuel confessed to the crime two years after his conviction for other killings.

**4 January 1964** Mary Sullivan, aged nineteen, was found murdered in her Boston apartment. It was to be the last murder attributed to the 'Boston Strangler'.

**6 January 1931** Miss Evelyn Foster, aged twenty-seven, was found badly burned beside her burnt-out taxi at a remote moorland spot known as Wolf's Neck, near Otterburn, Northumbria. The question remains did she torch the car for the insurance and burn herself in the process? Or was there, as she claimed before she succumbed to her burns, a male assailant who attacked her and set the car on fire?

**8 January 1914** Willie Starchfield, aged five, was sent on an errand and did not return. His body was found beneath the seat of a North London Railway train at Broad Street railway station. He had been strangled. The murder remains unsolved.

**10 January 1929** The decomposing body of Mr Vivian Messiter was found behind a garage in Southampton. He had been beaten to death with a hammer. Painstaking police and forensic work led to the arrest of fraudster William Henry Podmore, who was tried for the murder, found guilty and hanged at Winchester on 22 April 1930.

**13 January 1928** Earle Nelson, the 'Gorilla Murderer', responsible for the killing of twenty-two known victims, was hanged at the Vaughan Street Jail in Winnipeg, Canada.

**14 January 1862** Rebecca Law murdered her husband with over 100 cuts and slashes from a bill-hook, then killed her sixteen-week-old baby, Alfred, with a hammer at their home at Starlings Green in Clavering, Essex. She was removed to an asylum.

**17 January 1977** Double murderer Gary Gilmore was executed by firing squad at Utah State Prison in Draper, Utah, USA.

**18 January 1803** George Foster was hanged at Newgate for drowning his wife and child in Paddington Canal, London.

**20 January 1931** Julia Wallace was found beaten to death with a blunt object at her home in Wolverton Street, Liverpool. Her husband, William Herbert Wallace, who claimed he was out visiting a client and found her on his return, became a suspect. He was tried for her murder and was found guilty but won an appeal and was released. Wallace died in 1933. The case is still debated among crime historians.

**21 January 1958** Charles Starkweather killed Mr Marion and Mrs Velda Fugate and their daughter Betty Jean, aged two, at Lincoln, Nebraska, USA. He then left with Mr Fugate's stepdaughter, Caril Ann Fugate, and embarked on a cross-country killing spree.

**23 January 1931** Louisa Maud Steel, aged nineteen, set out on an errand from where she was in service on Lee Road, Blackheath. Her almost naked, mutilated body was found on the heath the following morning. No killer was ever brought to trial but senior investigating officers were satisfied that their number one suspect had been released from a mental institution to the care of his family shortly before the murder, and was put into a state institution immediately after.

**24 January 1907** William Whiteley, the founder of Whiteley's Department Store on Westbourne Grove, was shot dead at his shop by Horace Raynor, who claimed that he was Whiteley's illegitimate son.

**28 January 1905** Arthur Devereaux, aged twenty-four, a chemist's assistant of Kilburn, London, murdered his wife and twin sons by getting them to drink morphine. He hid their bodies in a trunk and had it removed to a commercial furniture store, before he moved to Coventry. He was hanged for the crime at Pentonville on 15 August 1905.

**31 January 1910** On or about this date, it was alleged that Dr Hawley Harvey Crippen murdered his wife, Cora, and buried some of her remains in the cellar of their home at No. 39 Hilldrop Crescent on Camden Road, Holloway, London.

# FEBRUARY

**1 February 1913** The bodies of Gustave Kunne and Elizabeth Warnes were discovered stabbed through the heart in the tea room of the Temperance Hotel, St Ives, Cambridgeshire. The evidence was not clear but it was certain no third person was involved. The coroner, clearly tiring of the enquiry, simplified the options for the jury, asking them to consider if the woman killed the man, vice versa, or did they commit suicide? The jury returned a verdict of murder and *felo de se* – Kunne murdered Warnes before committing suicide.

**2 February 1964** The body of Hannah Tailford, aged thirty, the first victim of still unidentified killer dubbed 'Jack the Stripper', was found in the Thames under a pier at Upper Mall, close to Hammersmith Bridge.

**3 February 1929** The five-minute murder trial. Joseph Clarke pleaded guilty to the murder of his landlady, Alice Fountaine. The judge asked if Clarke was certain and if he was aware of the consequences? Clarke said he was, so the judge donned the black cap and sentenced him to death.

**4 February 1929** The 'Madame 'X' Murder'. Mrs Kate Jackson was discovered by her husband laying a short distance from the back door of her home at Limeslade, near Swansea. She had been hit over the head and was removed to hospital, where she died from the injury a few days later. Investigations revealed she led a secret life as a blackmailer but her murderer was never identified.

**9 February 1942** Evelyn Hamilton was discovered strangled in an air-raid shelter in Montagu Place, in the Marylebone district of London. She was to prove to be the first victim of the 'Blackout Ripper', Gordon Cummings.

**10 February 1918** The body of Nellie Trew, aged sixteen, was found strangled on Eltham Common in London. David Greenwood was found guilty of the murder but his medical record from his service in the First World War showed he had suffered from shell shock. His appeal was granted and his sentence was altered to a life sentence.

**11 February 1897** The body of Walworth waitress Miss Annie Elizabeth Camp, aged thirty-three, was found pushed beneath a seat in compartment 2d on a London & South Western Railway train carriage at Waterloo Station, London. She had been beaten to death. Her murder remains unsolved.

**14 February 1929** Five of Bugs Moran's mobsters (and two others who got in the way) were gunned down by four still unknown assassins armed with Thompson sub-machine guns on the orders of Al Capone in the garage at 2122 North Clark Street, in the Lincoln Park neighbourhood of Chicago's North Side.

**16 February 1965** 'Jack the Stripper' victim, twenty-seven-year-old Bridie O' Hara, was found amongst a patch of bracken on the Heron Trading Estate in Acton, London.

**18 February 1949** The 'Acid Bath Murderer', John George Haigh, murdered Mrs Durand Deacon and attempted to destroy her body in a drum which he filled with sulphuric acid.

**19 February 1951** Jean Lee and her two accomplices, Robert Clayton and Norman Andrews, were hanged at Pentridge Jail in Coburg, Victoria, Australia for the violent murder of bookmaker William Kent, aged seventy-three, as they robbed him.

**21 February 1887** Grimsby fisherman Richard Insole was executed at Lincoln Prison. Insole was a volatile man who shot his wife five times (twice when she was on the floor), before stabbing himself in the groin. Sarah Insole died ten minutes later. Richard Insole recovered and was brought before the Lincoln Assizes where he was tried, found guilty and sentenced to death.

**22 February 1921** Mild-mannered solicitor Major Herbert Armstrong murdered his wife, Katherine, by poisoning her at their house Mayfield, in Hay-on-Wye, Hereford.

**23 February 1885** 'The Man They Could Not Hang.' John 'Babbacombe' Lee, was sentenced to death for the murder of Miss Emma Keyse, a crime he swore he did not commit. He was placed on the gallows traps three times at Exeter Prison – three times the traps did not fall. His sentence was commuted to life imprisonment.

**25 February 1922** Henri Désiré Landru, the French 'Bluebeard' serial killer of at least eleven women, was executed by guillotine in Versailles, France.

**26 February 1914** George Ball was executed at Walton Prison for beating his manager, Christina Bradfield, to death with a blunt instrument at the tarpaulin maker's shop where they worked on Old Hall Street, Liverpool.

# MARCH

**3 March 1903** Edgar Edwards, the man found guilty of the 'Camberwell Shop Murders' of Mr John Darby, his wife and their child, was hanged at Wandsworth by William Billington. Edwards' last words are recorded as, 'I have been looking forward to this lot.'

**6 March 1922** Ronald True murdered twenty-five-year-old prostitute Olive Young (real name Gertrude Yates) at her flat on Finborough Road in London.

**9 March 1966** London mobster George Cornell was shot and killed by Ronnie Kray at the Blind Beggar pub on Whitechapel Road in Whitechapel, London.

**10 March 1953** Miss Flora Gilligan, aged seventy-six, was found on the street outside her home in Diamond Street in York. She had been beaten to death and dropped from her bedroom window. Philip Henry was traced by the fingerprints and footprint he left behind him on the window. Tried at York Assizes, Henry was found guilty and was hanged at Armley Prison in Leeds on 30 July 1953.

**13 March 1929** The beaten and stabbed body of Mrs Winifred East, aged twenty-eight, was found on the Eltham to Kidbrooke railway line. A man aroused suspicion by running away from the train at Kidbrooke, but no murder was discovered until Mrs East was reported missing later that day and a search was undertaken. Her killer was never identified.

**14 March 1922** Lady Alice White, aged sixty-five, was found dying of head injuries at the Spencer Hotel on Portman Street, London. Eighteen-year-old pantry boy Henry Jacoby was found guilty and executed for the murder in June 1922.

**16 March 1903** The trial of George Chapman (born Severin Antoniovich Klosowski) opened at the Old Bailey. Found guilty of the murder of three women, he was hanged at Wandsworth on 7 April 1903.

**17 March 1780** Elizabeth Butchill was executed at Cambridge for the murder of her newborn daughter, who she dumped in the river near Trinity College bogs. After her execution, Butchill's body was ordered to be handed over to the anatomists for dissection.

**18 March 1910** John Nisbet, aged forty, was shot five times and his body hidden under the seat on the train which he usually caught from Newcastle, to take the wages to

Widdrington colliery. John Alexander Dickman was found guilty of the murder and was hanged at Newcastle Prison in August 1910.

**23 March 1935** Architect Francis Rattenbury was bludgeoned about the head with a carpenter's mallet and died from his injuries four days later. His wife confessed to the murder but her lover, the family chauffeur Percy Stoner, aged eighteen, claimed that he did it.

**24 March 1873** Executed at Durham Prison, Mrs Mary Ann Cotton had killed a number of her family, including three husbands, eight of her own children and seven stepchildren, in order to collect the insurance money paid out on their deaths.

# APRIL

**3 April 1924** Bank clerk William Hall was shot during a raid on a sub-branch in Bordon, Hampshire. The culprit, Abraham Goldberg, confessed after his arrest that he was attempting to get money quick so he could get married. Goldberg was hanged at Winchester Prison on 30 July 1924.

**4 April 1962** James Hanratty, convicted of the 'A6' murder, was executed by Harry Allen at Bedford Prison. Hanratty protested his innocence to the end.

**5 April 1936** Beatrice Vilna Sutton, aged forty-eight, was found suffocated at her flat in Clapham in London. Frederick Field was executed for the crime at Wandsworth Prison on 30 June. In his confession (which he later retracted) Field claimed he committed the murder because he was 'just browned off'.

**7 April 1779** Singer Martha Reay, mistress of the Earl of Sandwich, was shot and killed in Covent Garden by the ex-army officer and newly ordained Revd James Hackman, who had become infatuated with her.

**9 April 1964** 'Jack the Stripper' victim Irene Lockwood, aged twenty-six, was found on the foreshore in the Thames at Hammersmith, about 300 yards upstream from where the previous victim, Hannah Tailford, had been discovered in February.

**10 April 1955** Ruth Ellis shot David Blakely outside The Magdala Tavern in South Park Hill, Hampstead.

**12 April 1946** The body of Joyce Jacques, aged twenty-two, was found strangled on the foreshore of the beach at Morecambe in Lancashire. Walter Clayton, the man she had been seen out on a pub crawl that night, was traced and charged with her murder. At his trial at the Manchester Assizes, Clayton pleaded guilty. He was sentenced to death and hanged at Walton Prison on 7 August 1946.

**13 April 1850** The last public double execution at Cambridge Castle. Castle Camps farm labourer Elias Lucas, aged twenty-five, and his sister-in-law, twenty-year-old Mary Reeder, were hanged for the murder of Elias's wife, Susan, by the administration of two drams of arsenic.

**14 April 1949** The body of Emily Armstrong was found at the drycleaner's shop where she worked on St Jon's Wood High Street. She had been beaten to death. Her murder remains unsolved.

**15 April 1924** 'The Bungalow Murder'. Emily Kaye was murdered by Patrick Mahon in a bungalow on The Crumbles at Eastbourne. He then dismembered her body and hid most of it around the residence.

**16 April 1936** 'Nurse' Dorothea Waddingham, convicted murderer of Louisa Baguley, was executed at Winson Green Prison in Birmingham by Thomas Pierrepoint, assisted by his nephew, Albert Pierrepoint.

**24 April 1964** 'Jack the Stripper' victim Helene Barthelmy, aged twenty-two, was found in an alley off Swyncombe Avenue, near a sports ground in Brentford, West London.

**26 April 1999** BBC television presenter Jill Dando was shot and killed on the doorstep of her home in Fulham. Her murder remains unsolved.

**28 April 1919** Walter Cornish, aged forty-seven, his wife Alice, aged forty-three, and their two children, Alice, aged fourteen, and Marie, aged five, were beaten to death with an axe by Henry Perry at their home in Forest Gate, London. Perry was hanged by John Ellis and William Willis at Pentonville on 10 July 1919.

## MAY

**4 May 1735** Highwayman Dick Turpin shoots and kills Thomas Morris in Epping Forest. Morris was attempting to arrest the notorious outlaw and claim the reward for his capture.

**7 May 1896** American mass murderer H.H. Holmes (real name Herman Webster Mudgett) was hanged at Philadelphia's Moyamensing Prison.

**10 May 1927** A foul-smelling trunk deposited at the cloakroom at Charing Cross Station, London was opened, and the body of Minnie Bonati was discovered within. John Robinson was convicted and executed for this crime on 13 July the same year.

**11 May 1812** British Prime Minister Spencer Percival was assassinated in the lobby of the House of Commons by John Bellingham. Percival is the only British Prime Minister to have been assassinated.

**13 May 1833** Metropolitan Policeman PC Robert Culley, aged twenty-seven, died after being fatally stabbed during a political meeting on Coldbath Fields.

**18 May 1827** 'The Red Barn Murder'. William Corder murdered Maria Marten and buried her body in the dirt floor of the Red Barn in Polstead, Suffolk. When the murder was discovered, the case became one of the most notorious of the nineteenth century, as well as the subject of numerous books, broadsides and plays.

**19 May 1899** 'The Moat Farm Murder'. Samuel Herbert Dougal shot his lover, Miss Camille Holland, before hiding her body in the grounds of Moat Farm, Clavering, Essex.

**22 May 1870** John Owen (aka John Jones) murdered his master, blacksmith Emmanuel Marshall and six members of his family, in a frenzied hammer attack at Marshall's home in Denham, Middlesex. Owen had committed this horrible crime because he felt he had not been paid a fair wage. He was hanged at Aylesbury Gaol by William Calcraft on 8 August 1870.

**23 May 1892** Frederick Bailey Deeming, 'The Rainhill Murderer', was hanged at Melbourne Gaol, Australia.

**24 May 1934** Arthur Major was poisoned at his home in Kirkby-on-Bain, Lincolnshire. His wife, Ethel, was found guilty of the murder and was hanged at Hull Prison on 19 December.

**26 May 1868** The last man to be hanged in public in Great Britain was Michael Barrett, for his participation in the Clerkenwell Bombing that killed twelve people and injured many more. His execution was carried out by hangman William Calcraft in front of Newgate Prison, London.

**28 May 1932** The Tebbutt family of Meads End in Cambridge were planning to go on holiday; Mr Herbert Tebbutt had sent the servant girls out to wait in the car when they heard pistol shots inside the house. They rushed inside to find the three children and Mr Tebbutt's partner, Helen William, all dead. It was also apparent that having shot his family Mr Tebbutt then turned his pistol upon himself.

**31 May 1948** Mrs Minnie Freeman Lee, aged ninety-four, was found dead at her home in Maidenhead, Berkshire. She had been bound, gagged and battered about the head – she ultimately died of suffocation. George Russell was convicted of the murder and was hanged at Oxford Prison on 2 December 1948.

# JUNE

**1 June 1931** The charred remains of casual labourer Herbert 'Pigsticker' Ayres, aged forty-five, were discovered under a pile of smouldering rubbish at Scratchwood railway sidings near Elstree, Hertfordshire. He had been beaten to death with an axe. Oliver 'Tiggy' Newman, aged sixty-one, and William 'Moosh' Shelley, aged fifty-seven, were soon under arrest and a search of Newman's nearby shack turned up a bloody axe under the floorboards. Newman and Shelly were found guilty of the murder and executed in August 1931.

**5 June 1930** The body of twenty-year-old Agnes Kesson was discovered, dumped in a ditch on Horton Lane in Epsom, clothed only in her underwear and stockings. Forensic examination revealed she had been hit on the head with a blunt object and then strangled. Her murder remains unsolved.

**8 June 1946** Elizabeth McLindon was shot by her bigamist fiancé Arthur Robert Boyce with a .32 Browning automatic pistol in the house where she worked as a housekeeper at Chester Square, Belgravia, London. Boyce was hanged for the murder at Pentonville on 1 November 1946.

**10 June 1854** Mary Ann Brough murdered six of her eight children by cutting their throats with a razor at their home in Esher, Surrey. Found not guilty on grounds of insanity, she was detained 'until Her Majesty's pleasure be known'.

**11 June 1920** Society bridge expert and notorious philanderer Joseph Bowne Elwell, aged forty-four, was found slumped in his chair at his locked Manhattan home, dead from a single point-blank shot to his head from .45 revolver. Elwell's murder remains one of the notorious unsolved crimes of New York.

**12 June 1871** 'The Chocolate Cream Poisoner'. Sidney Albert Barker, aged four, died after visiting a Brighton sweet shop. Christiana Edmunds, aged forty-two, had started buying chocolates and lacing them with strychnine for some time before. There had been a number of instances of mysterious sickness striking people who received chocolates as presents, but Baker was the only fatality. Suspicion eventually fell on Edmunds; she was tried and sentenced to death but was reprieved because of her mental state. Sent to Broadmoor Criminal Lunatic Asylum, she died there in 1907.

**14 June 1946** Housekeeper Miss Elizabeth McLindon was found shot dead in the library of her employer's house in Chester Square, Belgravia. Her lover, petty criminal Arthur Boyce, was found guilty of her murder and was executed in November 1946.

**17 June 1928** Trevor Edwards murdered his pregnant sweetheart by cutting her throat with a razor in the Welsh mining village of Cynon Valley. He then slashed his own neck but did not to die from the wound. At his trial, Edwards pleaded insanity. The jury were not convinced and he was hanged at Swansea Prison on 11 December 1928.

**19 June 1928** The body of newlywed Siu Wai-Sheung was found strangled a short distance from the hotel where she and her husband were spending their honeymoon in the Lake District village of Grange-in-Borrowdale, Cumbria. Her husband, Chung Yi Miao, soon came under suspicion for her murder; he was tried, found guilty and hanged at Strangeways Prison at Manchester on 6 December 1928.

**20 June 1946** Margery Gardener was dancing in the evening at the Panama Club in South Kensington with sexual sadist Neville Heath. Her dead body was found in a Notting Hill hotel the following afternoon.

**21 June 1931** Lieutenant Hubert George Chevis died after eating a mouthful of one of a pair of partridges delivered to his home on Blackdown Camp in Aldershot, Hampshire. His killer and a motive for this murder remain unknown.

**22 June 1929** Alfred Oliver, aged sixty, was found badly wounded in his tobacconist shop on Cross Street, Reading; he died the following day. Actor Philip Yale Drew was appearing at a local theatre and was harangued at the inquest after two people believed they had seen him – or a man who looked like him – leaving the shop. Drew had nothing to do with the crime and the identity of the true murderer remains elusive.

**24 June 1926** Louis Calvert was hanged at Strangeways Prison in Manchester for beating and strangling Mrs Lily Waterhouse, her landlady, to death when she confronted Calvert about the theft of articles from her boarding house. When awaiting her fate in the condemned cell, Calvert confessed to the murder of John Frobisher, her previous employer, in 1922.

**25 June 1942** Twenty-eight-year-old Gordon Cummins, the 'Blackout Ripper', guilty of the murder of four women during the wartime blackouts in London, was executed at Wandsworth Prison by Albert Pierrepoint, assisted by Harry Kirk.

**28 June 1897** Israel Lipski kills Miriam Angel by forcing her to drink nitric acid in her bedroom at the house where they both rented rooms on Batty Street in Whitechapel, East London. Lipski was hanged for the murder at Newgate Prison on 21 August 1887.

# JULY

**5 July 1919** 'The Green Bicycle Mystery'. The body of Annie Bella Wright was found shot on the Gartree Road near Little Stretton, Leicestershire. Ronald Vivian Light was tried and acquitted of this crime.

**6 July 1910** Vaudeville performer Thomas Weldon Anderson (stage name Weldon Atherston) was found shot dead in an empty Battersea flat. His murder remains unsolved.

**8 July 1943** Millionaire Sir Harry Oakes was found brutally murdered at his mansion known as 'Westbourne' in Nassau, the Bahamas. Despite international press interest in the case, his killer was never identified and it remains the subject of debate and speculation among crime historians.

**9 July 1864** The first railway murder. Thomas Briggs was beaten and robbed by Franz Muller during the course of a robbery in the carriage he was travelling in while on the 9.50 p.m. North London Railway train between Fenchurch Street and Hackney Wick. Briggs died of the wounds he received soon after.

10 July 1909 Samuel Atherley cut the throats of his girlfriend, Matilda Lambert, and her three children with a razor at their home in Arnold, Nottingham. He then turned the razor on himself but survived. He was hanged for the murders at Nottingham on 14 December 1909.

**11 July 1958** Peter Manuel, vicious robber, sex attacker, rapist and serial murderer, was hanged at Barlinnie Prison, Glasgow.

**12 July 1866** Dr Alfred William Warden drank prussic acid in his room in the Bedford Hotel to avoid arrest, following the death of his wife from aconite poisoning at their home in Brighton, East Sussex. His previous two wives had also died in mysterious circumstances.

**13 July 1955** Ruth Ellis, aged twenty-eight, was executed at Holloway Prison by Albert Pierrepoint. She was the last woman to be hanged in Great Britain.

**14 July 1964** 'Jack the Stripper' victim Mary Fleming, aged thirty, was found dead in a sitting position outside the entrance to a garage in Berrymede Road, Acton.

**15 July 1953** John Reginald Halliday Christie, the notorious serial killer of 10 Rillington Place, was executed at Pentonville by Albert Pierrepoint.

**23 July 1943** 'The Bath Chair Murder'. Mr Archibald Brown was blown up while his nurse was taking him out along the London Road in Rayleigh, Essex. The cause of the explosion had been a Hawkins mine that had been planted in his wheelchair by his son, Eric.

**28 July 1926** The body of Edwin Creed, aged forty-six, was discovered on the cellar stairs of the cheesemonger's where he was manager, on Leinster Terrace just off Bayswater Road in Lancaster Gate, London. He had been beaten to death, probably with a 'jemmy' or crowbar. Traces of blood in the sawdust on the shop floor showed he had been attacked there and his body dragged to the cellar stairs and thrown down them. Descriptions of two men seen changing their clothes and leaving their old ones behind at a public baths were circulated but to no avail. The murder of Edwin Creed remains unsolved.

# AUGUST

**3 August 1931** Mrs Annie Louise Kempson was found battered to death with a hammer and a chisel gouge to her throat at her home in St Clements Street, Oxford. Henry Seymour was executed for the murder at Oxford Prison on 10 December 1931.

**6 August 1819** Thomas Weems was executed for the murder of his wife, Mary Ann, in front of a huge crowd at the County Gaol, Cambridge. After hanging for an hour, Weems' body was cut down and removed to the Chemical Lecture Room in the Botanical Garden, where Professor Cumming performed experiments upon it using electrical current generated from a powerful galvanic battery.

**9 August 1967** Playwright Joe Orton was murdered by his lover Kenneth Halliwell at the home they shared on Noel Road, Islington. Halliwell then took his own life with an overdose of Nembutal tablets.

**10 August 1893** Cecil Hambrough was shot and killed in mysterious circumstances during a shooting expedition with two other men, on an estate at Ardlamont in Argyllshire, Scotland.

**12 August 1966** 'The Massacre of Braybrook Street'. Three plainclothes CID officers were killed while questioning three criminals parked on a housing estate a short distance from Wormwood Scrubs Prison, London. A manhunt ensued and the suspects, John Edward 'Jack' Witney, John Duddy and Harry Maurice Roberts, were all arrested and sentenced to life imprisonment.

**13 August 1964** 'The Last to Hang'. Murderer Gwynne Owen Evans was hanged by executioner Harry Allen at Strangeways Prison, Manchester, and Peter Allen was hanged at Walton Prison, Liverpool, by Robert Leslie Stewart at 8 a.m. Both men were executed for the murder of John West during a robbery on 7 April 1964.

**14 August 1926** The body of retired farmer Hilary Rougier, aged seventy-seven, was found in the room he rented in a large house called 'Nuthurst', in Woking. He had died of morphine poisoning and the coroner's jury were convinced Rougier had not administered it to himself. The murder of Hilary Rougier remains unsolved.

**15 August 1875** Frederick Page, aged twenty, murdered servant girl Fanny Clarke by shooting and beating her to death in Brantham, Suffolk. Brought before the County Assizes, Page was found guilty but insane and ordered to be detained at Her Majesty's pleasure.

**16 August 1830** Metropolitan Policeman PC John Long, aged thirty-five, was murdered on duty. He was stabbed to death when he stopped three suspected burglars in Gray's Inn Lane.

**19 August 1922** Thomas Allaway was executed at Winchester Prison for beating Irene Wilkins to death with a heavy car spanner after an unsuccessful attempt to rape her.

**20 August 1921** 'The Crumbles Murder'. The brutally murdered body of seventeen-year-old Irene Munro was discovered on 'the Crumbles' at Eastbourne. A pair of out of work ne're-do-wells, William Thomas Gray, aged twenty-nine, and Jack Alfred Field, aged nineteen, were executed for the killing.

**24 August 1908** Mrs Caroline Luard was found shot dead on the veranda of the summerhouse in the grounds of her house at Ightham, Kent. Despite having a cast-iron alibi, suspicion still fell upon her elderly husband, retired Major General Charles Luard. He could not stand the lingering rumours and threw himself under a train. Caroline Luard's murderer was never brought to justice.

**26 August 1961** 'The A6 Murder'. Michael Gregsten was shot and killed and Valerie Storie was raped, shot and left for dead at Deadman's Hill near Clophill, Bedfordshire on the A6, after a nightmare carjacking. James Hanratty was executed for the crime at Bedford Prison on 4 April 1962.

**29 August 1948** The body of Nancy Chadwick was found dumped on a roadside at Rawtenstall, Lancashire. She had been beaten to death with a hammer. Margaret Allen was executed for the murder at Strangeways Prison on 12 January 1949.

**31 August 1888** Mary Ann 'Polly' Nichols, first of the canonical five victims of Jack the Ripper, was found lying on the ground by a gated entrance on Buck's Row (now known as Durward Street) in Whitechapel, London.

# SEPTEMBER

**1 September 1827** Joshua Slade, aged eighteen, was executed upon the Huntingdon Gallows for the murder of the Revd Joshua Waterhouse, aged eighty-one, when he tried to rob him at Little Stukeley rectory. Slade's body was handed to the anatomists; his skin was flayed from his corpse, tanned and sold as grim souvenirs, while his skeleton went for display in a travelling show.

**5 September 1930** Thirty-nine-year-old Carl Panzram, American serial killer, homosexual rapist, arsonist and burglar, convicted of twenty-two murders, was hanged at Fort Leavenworth, Kansas. When asked by the executioner if he had any last words, Panzram snapped back, 'Yes, hurry it up, you Hoosier bastard! I could kill ten men while you're fooling around!'

**6 September 1933** The body of wealthy cattle dealer Frederick Morton was recovered from the wreckage of his burnt-out garage at Saxton Grange, near Towton in Yorkshire. He had been shot in the chest. Ernest Brown, Morton's disgruntled former groom, was found guilty of the murder and was executed at Armley Prison in Leeds on 6 February 1934.

**8 September 1888** Annie Chapman become the second of the canonical five victims of Jack the Ripper. Her body was discovered shortly before 6 a.m. in the backyard of No. 29 Hanbury Street in Spitalfields, London.

**11 September 1907** 'The Camden Town Murder'. Part-time prostitute Emily Dimmock was found murdered at her home on St Paul's Road, Camden. Robert Wood was tried and acquitted of the crime.

**14 September 1911** Miss Eliza Barrow died from arsenic poisoning in the house where she lodged at Tollington Park, North London. Frederick Seddon, the man who had befriended her and had already wrung a considerable amount of money out of her, was found guilty of her murder and hanged for it in April 1912.

**17 September 1956** Mother and daughters Marion Watt, aged forty-five, Vivienne Watt, aged seventeen, and Marion's sister, Margaret Brown, aged forty-one, were found shot dead in their home in Burnside, Glasgow. Peter Manuel was convicted of their murder and executed in 1958.

**20 September 1930** Miss Margery Wren, aged eighty-two, was found badly beaten after a robbery at her shop on Church Road in Ramsgate, Kent. She was removed to hospital where she made a number of confused statements. Shortly before she died she was asked to name her murderer. She replied, 'I don't want him to suffer. He must bear his sins. I don't wish to make a statement.' Her murderer has never been identified.

**21 September 1953** 'The Body in the Crypt'. The body of Mary Hackett, aged six, was found in a space between the foundations and the floor of Park Congregational Church in Halifax, Yorkshire – a building just 150 yards from her home. Church caretaker, George Albert Hall, was found guilty of the murder and was hanged at Leeds Prison in April 1954.

**23 September 1900** The body of Mary Jane Bennett was found strangled with a bootlace on the beach at Great Yarmouth, Norfolk. Her husband, Herbert Bennett, was hanged for the murder in 1901, but the question of his guilt or innocence is still debated.

**24 September 1930** Warsop provision merchant Samuel Fell Wilson was found dead in his delivery van. He had received a shot in the shoulder from a 12 bore shotgun. The van ploughed into the verge of Forest Road, halfway between Clipstone and Market Warsop, Mansfield, Nottinghamshire. The killer then walked over and fired again at point-blank range, killing Wilson instantly. Detectives could find neither motive nor suspect and the murder remains unsolved.

**26 September 1947** Catherine McIntyre was found bound, gagged and battered to death at her home in Kenmore, Perthshire, Scotland. Polish soldier Stanislaw Myszka was hanged for the crime at Perth on 6 February 1948.

**27 September 1927** The body of PC Gutteridge was found shot dead in a country lane between Romford and Ongar in Essex. Frederick Guy Browne and William Kennedy were hanged at separate prisons for the killing on 31 May 1928.

**29 September 1935** The bodies of Mrs Isabella Ruxton and nursemaid Mary Jane Rogerson were discovered dismembered under the bridge crossing Gardenholm Linn, a tributary of the River Annan near Moffat, Scotland.

**30 September 1888** 'The Double Event'. Elizabeth 'Long Liz' Stride and Catherine 'Kate' Eddowes become the third and fourth (of the canonical five) victims of Jack the Ripper. Stride was killed in Dutfield's Yard, off Berner Street, Whitechapel, and Eddowes in Mitre Square, City of London.

# OCTOBER

**1 October 1887** The Revd William Meymott Farley, the seventy-three-year-old Rector of Cretingham in Suffolk, was murdered in his bed by his Curate, Revd A.E. Gilbert-Cooper, who wielded a cut-throat razor on his elderly victim. Found guilty but insane, Gilbert-Cooper was sent to Broadmoor Prison Asylum for the rest of his life.

**2 October 1883** 'The Black Widows of Liverpool'. Thomas Higgins, aged forty-five, died of arsenic poisoning. His wife, Margaret, and her sister, Catherine Flannagan, had poisoned him to collect the death benefit paid on his demise. Both women were found guilty of murder and were hanged on 3 March 1884 at Kirkdale Prison, Liverpool. It was suspected the early deaths of a number of other family members had been caused by these women.

**3 October 1922** Thirty-four-year-old Percy Thompson and his wife, Edith, aged thirty-two, were walking back to their Ilford home when Edith's lover, Frederick Bywaters, aged twenty-one, stepped out from the shadows and attacked Mr Thompson. A struggle ensued, leaving Thompson mortally wounded. Bywaters swore Mrs Thompson was not complicit in the murder but the jury were not convinced and the pair went to the gallows.

**4 October 1869** Frederick Hinson was convinced that his lover, Maria Death, was having an affair with a man named William Boyd. After a failed attack on the pair, near Wood Green Station, Hinson ran off. Later he found Death, shot her and beat her with the pistol, then tracked down Boyd and shot him too. Hinson was captured after he attempted to cut his own throat. He was hanged for the murders outside Newgate on 13 December 1869.

**7 October 1942** 'The Wigwam Murder'. The decomposing body of Joan Wolfe, aged nineteen, was found on Hankley Common in Godalming, Surrey. She had been beaten to death with a wooden stake. French-Canadian soldier August Sangret was found guilty of the murder and was executed at Wandsworth Prison on 29 April 1943.

**8 October 1871** Classics lecturer and author Revd John Selby Watson beat his wife to death with the butt of his pistol. Watson pleaded insanity but was found guilty of murder. Sentenced to death, he was reprieved and sent to Parkhurst, where he spent the rest of his life until his death in 1884.

**9 October 1912** George Mackay (aka John Williams) shot Police Inspector Arthur Walls when he challenged Mackay about his suspicious behaviour in the shadows around the portico of Countess Flora Sztaray at her home on South Cliff Avenue, Eastbourne. Mackay was found guilty and was hanged at Lewes Gaol by John Ellis in January 1913.

**14 October 1941** Mrs Theodora Greenhill, aged sixty-five, was found murdered in the drawing room of her flat on Elsham Road in West Kensington, London. She had been struck on the head with a beer bottle and strangled. Harold Dorian Trevor, an elegant monocle-wearing fraudster and thief, was hanged for the killing at Wandsworth on 11 March 1942.

**16 October 1953** John and Phoebe Harries were last seen alive at their farm at Llanginning, near St Clears, Carmarthenshire. Their adopted nephew, Ronald, explained their disappearance by claiming they had gone to London on holiday, leaving him to look after the farm. Three weeks later their murdered bodies were found buried in one of the fields. Ronald Harries was tried and found guilty of the murder of his aunt and uncle and was executed at Swansea Prison in April 1954.

**18 October 1947** 'The Porthole Murder'. Actress Gay Gibson (real name Eileen Isabella Ronnie Gibson) was believed to have been murdered and her body disposed of by pushing it through the porthole of the Union Castle liner *Durban Castle*, as it sailed from Cape Town to Southampton. Gay's body was never recovered. Ship steward James Camb was tried and found guilty of the murder but his death sentence was commuted to life imprisonment.

**20 October 1862** Nurse Catherine Wilson was hanged in front of Newgate Prison, London for the murder of one of her patients. It was believed by many that she had been responsible for the death of a further six. Her execution drew a crowd in excess of 20,000.

**21 October 1949** A torso identified as that of fraudster Stanley Setty was found on the marshes near Tillingham in Essex. Brian Donald Hume had hired a sports plane and was suspected of having dumped the body parts as he flew over the marshes. Tried for the murder of Setty, Hume was acquitted of murder but found guilty of being an accessory to the crime and was sentenced to twelve years. After his release, Hume was paid £2,000 by the *Sunday Pictorial* for his confession that he had killed Setty.

**23 October 1929** Swindler Sidney Harry Fox murdered his mother, Mrs Rosalie Fox, at the Metropole Hotel in Margate, Kent.

**24 October 1823** John Thurtell shot William Weare over gambling debts in Radlett, Hertfordshire. The case was notorious in its day and was the subject of books, broadsides and plays.

**27 October 1919** New Orleans grocer Mike Pepitone was found brutally murdered at his home. He is believed to have been the last victim of the killer dubbed the 'Axeman of New Orleans'.

**31 October 1946** The body of spinster Dagmar Peters, aged forty-seven, was found in shrubbery at Wrotham Hill in Kent – she had been strangled. Scotland Yard investigator DCI Robert Fabian was convinced Harold Haggar, an ex-prisoner delivery driver, who admitted under questioning that he had given Miss Peters a lift, was guilty of her murder, despite appearing to have no motive to kill her. Haggar was tried, found guilty and hanged at Wandsworth in March 1947.

## NOVEMBER

**1 November 2006** Russian dissident and ex-Russian Secret Service agent Alexander Litvinenko was poisoned with radioactive polonium-210. He died at University College Hospital two days later. At the time of writing, his death remains a mystery.

**4 November 1930** Mrs Alice Thomas of Trenhorne Farm in Lewannick, Cornwall died at a hospital in Plymouth. A quantity of arsenic was found in her body. Her neighbour, Mrs Annie Hearn of Trehorne House, was tried for the murder at Bodmin Assizes – the jury found Mrs Hearn innocent and the murder remains unsolved.

**5 November 1959** Petty thief Guenther Podola was executed at Wandsworth Prison and became the last man to hang in Britain for shooting a police officer. He had shot Detective Sergeant Raymond Purdy in the heart as the officer attempted to arrest him in Kensington, London.

**6 November 1930** 'The Blazing Car Murder'. An unidentified body was discovered after the fire was put out in a torched car on Hardingstone Lane, about three miles from Northampton. It had been an attempt by Alfred Arthur Rouse to fake his own death and start a new life under a new identity. He was hanged for the murder at Bedford in March 1931. His confession was later published in the *Daily Sketch,* but the identity of the body in the blazing car remains a mystery.

**7 November 1952** Miles Giffard, aged twenty-six, shot both his parents at the large home he shared with them on the cliffs overlooking Carlyon Bay near St Austell, Cornwall. Giffard claimed, 'I can only say I must have had a brainstorm'. A pair of Home Office psychiatrists declared him sane and he was tried, found guilty and hanged at Horfield Prison in Bristol on 24 February 1953.

**9 November 1888** Many Jane Kelly was claimed as the fifth and final victim of Jack the Ripper. Her horribly mutilated body was discovered by Thomas Bowyer, who had been sent to collect her rent at 13 Miller's Court off Dorset Street, Spitalfields.

**10 November 1902** Emma 'Kitty' Byron had had enough of the way she was abused and the assaults she received from Arthur Baker, the man she lived with. When a fight between the pair spilled out onto the street near their lodgings in London, Byron stabbed Baker twice. Found guilty of murder she was sentenced to death, this was commuted to life imprisonment, a sentence reduced to ten years in 1907, of which she served six.

**11 November 1921** Annie Black died from arsenic poisoning at her home at Tregonissey in Cornwall. Her husband, Edward, was found in Liverpool after he had attempted to commit suicide. Tried for the murder of his wife, he was found guilty and hanged at Exeter Prison on 24 March 1922.

**15 November 1892** Thomas Neill Cream, the 'Lambeth Poisoner', was hanged at Newgate Prison by executioner James Billington.

**18 November 1943** 'The Luton Sack Murder'. Caroline Manton was murdered, put in a sack and dumped in the River Lea in Luton by her husband, Horace William 'Bertie' Manton.

**19 November 1971** Fred Biggs died, another victim of the mysterious 'Bovingdon Bug' – in reality, he was one of a number of people on the staff of a local business who had been poisoned with thallium by their murderous storeman Graham Young.

**21 November 1931** Peter Queen strangled Chrissie Gall with a washing line. They had lived together as husband and wife on Dumbarton Road in Glasgow for almost a year, but she had taken to drinking and had attempted suicide on a number of occasions. Despite concerns voiced by pathologists Spilsbury and Smith that she had committed suicide, the jury decided Queen had strangled Gall and he was sentenced to death. The sentence was, however, commuted to life imprisonment.

**22 November 1941** The bodies of Kathleen Trendle, aged six, and Doreen Joyce Hearne, aged eight, were found in Penn

Wood, Buckinghamshire. Both girls had been stabbed to death. A gas mask container found nearby was fingerprinted and led to a serviceman named Harold Hill, aged twenty-six. Hill pleaded insanity but was found guilty of their murder and was hanged at Oxford Castle on 1 May 1942.

**23 November 1910** Dr Hawley Harvey Crippen, aged forty-eight, was hanged at Pentonville Prison in London by executioner John Ellis. Crippen had been found guilty of the murder of his wife, Cora. Always keen to point out his mistress was completely innocent, he never actually confessed to the crime.

**24 November 1862** PC Ebenezer Tye, aged twenty-four, was found badly beaten and drowned in a sewage-laden stream at the rear of Chediston Street in Halesworth, Suffolk. Local hardman John Ducker, aged sixty-three, bragged to a local chimneysweep that he had 'done for' Tye. Tried and found guilty of the murder, Ducker was executed at Ipswich on 14 April 1863 and has the dubious distinction of being the last man to be hanged in public in Suffolk.

**25 November 1964** 'Jack the Stripper' victim, twenty-one-year-old Margaret McGowan (aka Frances Brown), was found hidden under rubble and a dustbin lid in a car park on Hornton Street, Kensington.

**30 November 1946** The body of John Mudie was found in Woldingham Chalk Pit in Surrey. He had been tortured and his body dumped. Former Australian politician Thomas Ley had suspected his mistress of having an affair with Mudie, and with the help of two accomplices meted out this punishment upon him. Ley was sent to Broadmoor where he died a few months later.

# DECEMBER

**3 December 1881** Percy John died at Blenheim House School, Wimbledon after his uncle, Dr George Henry Lamson, gave him a slice of Dundee cake laced with aconite.

**5 December 1924** Norman Thorne murdered Elsie Cameron, his no-longer-wanted sweetheart, and buried her under the chicken run at his small poultry farm at Crowborough in East Sussex.

**8 December 1957** Newcastle taxi driver Sydney Dunn was found, having been shot and his throat cut, on the moors at Edmondbyers in County Durham. The man named as the perpetrator of the crime by a coroner's inquest was multiple murderer Peter Manuel, and he was executed in July 1958.

**10 December 1951** Herbert Mills was executed for the murder of Mabel Tattershaw, who he hit with a blunt object then strangled in a Nottingham orchard in an attempt to commit 'the perfect murder'.

**14 December 1931** Eleven-year-old Vera Page was reported missing by her father. Her body was found two days later, dumped in bushes by Addison Road, Holland Park, London; she had been raped and strangled. There was a prime suspect for the murder but no witness had seen him with Vera on the day of her murder, although the account he gave of his movements at the inquest were unverified, he was not charged with the crime.

**17 December 1914** George Joseph Smith drowned Margaret Lofty, the last of his 'brides', in a bath at Highgate in London.

**21 December 1908** Miss Marion Gilchrist, aged eighty-two, was found beaten to death at her home on Queen's Terrace, West Prince's Street, Glasgow. Oscar Slater was convicted of the murder on circumstantial evidence; his death sentence was commuted and despite compelling campaigns for a re-examination of the case, including a re-examination of the circumstances of the case by Sherlock Holmes creator Sir Arthur Conan Doyle, it was eighteen years before it was re-examined and Slater was set free.

**22 December 1935** Frederick Bryant died in agony after being given a cup of steaming Oxo laced with arsenic by his wife, Charlotte, at Over Compton in Dorset. Tried and found guilty of her husband's murder she was hanged at Exeter Prison on 15 July 1936.

**24 December 1867** Frederick Baker was hanged outside Winchester Gaol for the murder of sweet Fanny Adams.

**28 December 1957** Isabelle Cooke, aged seventeen, disappeared after attending a dance at Uddingston Grammar School in South Lanarkshire, Scotland. Her killer, Peter Manuel, led police to the field near the school where he had buried her.

## TRUE-CRIME BUFF'S BOOKSHELF

The following are some of the essential British true-crime authors and some of their books:

Major Arthur Griffiths, *Mysteries of Police and Crime* (3 volumes) (Cassell, 1902)

Camden Pelham, *The Chronicles of Crime Or the New Newgate Calendar* (2 volumes) (Miles & Co., 1887)

Harry Furniss, *Famous Crimes* – a part work published from 1903

Richard Whittington-Egan, *The Bedside Book of Murder* (David and Charles, 1988)

William Roughead, *Chronicles of Murder* (Lochar 1991)

Richard and Molly Whittington-Egan, *Murder on File: The World's Most Notorious Killer* (Wilson, 2005)

Edgar Lustgarten, *The Murder and the Trial* (Odhams, 1960)

_____*The Business of Murder* (Harrap, 1968)

Hargrave L. Adam, *Murder Most Mysterious* (Sampson Low, 1932)

Donald Rumbelow, *The Houndsditch Murders and the Siege of Sidney Street* (The History Press, 2008)

_____ *The Complete Jack the Ripper* (The History Press, 2010)

Stewart P. Evans, *The Lodger* (Random House, 1995)

_____ *Jack the Ripper: The Ultimate Sourcebook* (with Keith Skinner) (Robinson, 2002)

_____ Stuart P. Evans, *Jack the Ripper: Letters from Hell* (The History Press, 2004)

*Jack the Ripper: Scotland Yard Investigates* (with Donald Rumbelow) (The History Press, 2006)

Colin Wilson, *A Casebook of Murder* (Mayflower, 1971)

_____ *Encyclopaedia of Modern Murder* (Book Club Associates, 1984)

_____ *The Mammoth Book of True Crime* (Robinson, 1988)

Sir Francis Camps, *Camps on Crime* (David and Charles, 1973)

Sir Sydney Smith, *Mostly Murder* (Harrap, 1959)

Douglas G. Browne, *Bernard Spilsbury: His Life and Cases* (Harrap, 1952)

Edward Marjoribanks, *For the Defence: The Life of Sir Edward Marshall Hall* (Macmillan, 1929)

Martin Fido, *Murders After Midnight* (Orion, 1993)

_____ *The Chronicle of Crime* (Carlton, 2000)

_____ *A History of British Serial Killing* (Carlton, 2003)

Paul Begg, Martin Fido & Keith Skinner, *The Complete Jack the Ripper A to Z* (Blake, 2010)

Martin Fido & Keith Skinner, *The Scotland Yard Files: 150 Years of the CID* (Headline, 1992)

_____ *Jack the Ripper: CSI Whitechapel* (Andre Deutsch, 2012)

J.H.H. Gaute & Robin Odell, *The Murderer's Who's Who* (Pan, 1980)

_____ *Murder 'Whatdunit'* (Harrap, 1982)

_____ *Murder 'Whereabouts'* (Leisure Circle, 1986)

Philip Sugden, *The Complete History of Jack the Ripper* (Robinson, 1995)

Jonathan Goodman, *The Lady Killers: Famous Women Murderers* (Time Warner, 1991)

_____ *The Giant Book of Murder* (Paragon, 1997)

_____ *Masterpieces of Murder* (Constable, 2005)

Brian Lane, *The Murder Guide* (Robinson, 1991)

_____ *Chronicle of Murder* (2004)

_____ *Murder Club Guide* series for across Great Britain

Gordon Honeycombe, *Murders of The Black Museum* (Arrow, 1984)

_____ *More Murders of the Black Museum* (Hutchinson, 1994)

Neil R. Storey, *Prisons and Prisoners in Victorian Britain* (The History Press, 2010)

_____ *The Victorian Criminal* (Shire, 2011)

*The Grim Almanac* series (The History Press)

John J. Eddlestone, *The Encyclopaedia of Executions* (Blake, 2003)


It should also be noted that no true-crime buff should be without a copy of their favourite cases as covered (by various authors) in the *Notable Scottish Trials* (NST), *Notable English Trials* (NET) and *Notable British Trials* (NBT) series, published by William Hodge & Company Ltd between 1905 and 1959. There are over eighty titles in the complete series.


## SOME CINEMA AND TV FILMS BASED ON TRUE MURDER CASES

*M* (Peter Kürten, 'The Vampire of Dusseldorf') 1931

*Rope* (Leopold and Leob) 1948

*The Case of Charles Peace* (Charles Peace, 'The Banner Cross Murderer') 1949

*Psycho* (Ed Gein) 1960

*Dr Crippen* (Dr Hawley Harvey Crippen) 1962

*The Boston Strangler* (Albert DeSalvo, the 'Boston Strangler') 1968

*Conceptions of Murder: Conversation Piece* (Miles Giffard, 'The Carlyon Bay Murders') 1970

*10, Rillington Place* (John Christie) 1971

*Who Killed Julia Wallace?* (William Herbert Wallace) 1975

*The Town That Dreaded Sundown* (The unsolved 'Texarkana Moonlight Murders') 1976

*The Crumbles Murder* (Patrick Mahon) 1976

*Dance with a Stranger* (Ruth Ellis) 1985

*Jack the Ripper* (Jack the Ripper) 1988

*Chicago Joe and the Showgirl* (Karl Hulten and Georgina Grayson (real name Elizabeth Jones)) 1990

*The Krays* (Ronald and Reginald Kray) 1990

*Let Him Have It* (Derek Bentley and Christopher Craig) 1991

*To Catch a Killer* (John Wayne Gacy) 1992

*The Young Poisoner's Handbook* (Graham Young) 1995

*The Life and Crimes of William Palmer* (William Palmer, the 'Rugeley Poisoner') 1998

*From Hell* (Jack the Ripper) 2001

*A is for Acid* (John Haigh, the 'Acid Bath Murderer') 2002

*Dahmer* (Jeffrey Dahmer) 2002

*The Brides in the Bath* (George Joseph Smith, 'The Brides in the Bath' murderer) 2003

*Gacy* (John Wayne Gacy) 2003

*Helter Skelter* (Charles Manson and the Manson 'family') 2003

*Monster* (Eileen Wuornos) 2003

*The Black Dahlia* (the unsolved murder of Elizabeth Short, the 'Black Dahlia') 2006

*Zodiac* (the unsolved killings of the murder who dubbed himself 'Zodiac') 2007

*Snowtown* (John Bunting, 'The Bodies in Barrels Murders' in South Australia) 2011

*Appropriate Adult* (Fred and Rosemary West) 2011

# ACKNOWLEDGEMENTS

Any attempt at a bibliography for this book would result in a very unwieldy list of publications, but I would like to extend thanks to the team of experts and friends who have made suggestions for subjects and cases to research and include, helped check facts and endured my obsession with the strange and the obscure: Stewart P. Evans and his good lady, Rosie, Andrew Selwyn-Crome, James Nice, Martin Sercombe, Britta Pollmuller, Martin and Pip Faulks, Rebecca Matthews, Fergus and Anne Roy, Ian Pycroft, Dr Geoffrey Clayton, Dr Vic Morgan, Michael Bean, Lynsey Frary, Helen Radlett, Michelle Bullivant, Steve and Eve Bacon, Christine and David Parmenter, Neil Bell, Lindsay Siviter, The Galleries of Justice in Nottingham, Thames Valley Police Museum, Lincoln Castle, Norfolk Police Archive, The Library of the University of East Anglia, my darling Molly and son Lawrence.

If you enjoyed this book, you may also be interested in …

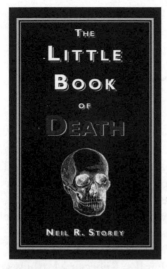

## The Little Book of Death

NEIL R. STOREY

This little book is a repository of intriguing, fascinating, obscure, strange and entertaining facts and trivia about the one certainty in all our lives – death. Within this volume are some horrible, unfortunate and downright ludicrous ends. Learn of odd last requests, burials, epitaphs and death rites from around the world, and a whole host of horrible tales about mummies, vampires, zombies, auto-icons and body-snatchers. Anyone brave enough to read this book will be entertained and enthralled and never short of some frivolous fact to enhance a conversation or quiz!

978 0 7524 7151 8

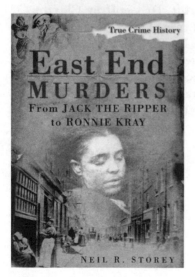

## East End Murders: From Jack the Ripper to Ronnie Kray

NEIL R. STOREY

As well as the murders of Jack the Ripper, perhaps the most infamous in history, Neil R. Storey looks at nine other cases in detail, including the still mysterious Ratcliffe Highway Murders of 1811; Henry Wainwright, who dismembered his mistress and rolled up her remains in a carpet in 1874; the unsolved murder of Frances Coles in 1891; the Whitechapel High Street Newspaper Shop Murder in 1904, and the shooting of George Cornell by Ronnie Kray at the Blind Begger pub in 1966. *East End Murders* is a unique re-examination of the darker side of the capital's past.

978 0 7524 5069 5